BOLLINGEN SERIES XLVI

MIRCEA ELIADE

The MYTH of the ETERNAL RETURN

COSMOS AND HISTORY

Translated from the French by

Willard R. Trask

With a new introduction by

Jonathan Z. Smith

BOLLINGEN SERIES XLVI

PRINCETON UNIVERSITY PRESS

PRINCETON AND OXFORD

Originally published in French as
Le Mythe de l'éternel retour: archétypes et répétition
by Librairie Gallimard, NRF, Paris, 1949

Published in Harper Torchbooks paperback edition
(New York, 1959) under the title *Cosmos and History*

Second printing, with corrections, 1965

First Princeton / Bollingen paperback edition, 1971

Second paperback edition, with a new introduction by Jonathan Z. Smith, 2005

THIS IS THE FORTY-SIXTH IN A SERIES OF WORKS
SPONSORED BY BOLLINGEN FOUNDATION

Library of Congress Control Number 2004117650

ISBN 0-691-12350-0

ISBN-13: 978-0-691-12350-9 (pbk.)

British Library Cataloging-in-Publication Data is available

Printed on acid-free paper. ∞

pup.princeton.edu

Printed in the United States of America

9 10 8

TO

Tantzi AND Brutus Coste

in Memory of our Evenings

at the Chalet Chaimite

*

CONTENTS

CONTENTS

INTRODUCTION TO THE 2005 EDITION

by Jonathan Z. Smith

IN 1954, Mircea Eliade's first important book to be published in English appeared: *The Myth of the Eternal Return.* Translated by Willard R. Trask, it was the forty-sixth volume in the distinguished Bollingen Series, originally published by Kurt Wolff's Pantheon Press and, after 1967, continued by Princeton University Press. Eliade was forty-seven, the author of some fifty books (chiefly in Romanian), then living in Paris in desperately straitened circumstances. Eliade had met John (Jack) Barrett, the editor of the series, on August 25, 1950, during Eliade's first appearance at the Jungian circle's annual Eranos conference in Ascona, Switzerland. Barrett made possible both the subsequent publication of the translation, and, more immediately, Eliade's grant of a Bollingen Foundation Fellowship for three years, which would enable him to continue his research at a stipend of two hundred dollars per month. The 1954 translation sold more than 100,000 copies by 1982 and established Eliade's North American reputation, which was made secure by his appointment to the faculty of the University of Chicago in 1956–57, his first regular academic position.

Eliade appears to have begun thinking about this book in 1944 while stationed at the Romanian embassy in Lisbon, Portugal. He notes in his journal toward the end of January of that year, "I should like to write about the 'terror of history.'" The actual writing of the Romanian manuscript, as well as its translation into French by Jean

Gouillard and Jacques Soucasse, took place during 1945–47, often interspersed with other projects, most especially the drafting of the large volume later published in English translation under the title *Patterns in Comparative Religion* (1958). *Myth* was originally entitled *Cosmos and History*; changed first to *Archetypes and Repetition* (now the title of the first chapter), and then, in its initial French edition, to *The Myth of the Eternal Return: Archetypes and Repetition* (1949). The English translation now before you is a revised version of this French original. The majority of these revisions were subsequently incorporated into the 1969 second French edition.

None of these titles, with the possible exception of *Archetypes and Repetition*, quite captures Eliade's own sense of the double agendum of his work as described in a journal entry from October 3, 1949: "More than any other critic, [Eugenio] d'Ors is enthusiastic because I have brought out the Platonic structure of archaic and traditional ('folk') ontologies. But I am still waiting for the other side of my interpretation to be understood, that concerning the ritual abolition of time and, hence, the necessity of 'repetition.'" Neither the titles nor this self-description give voice to perhaps the most startling element of the book in its later chapters, a development of the consequences of this "abolition of time," namely Eliade's fierce polemics against a modernist faith in history as a progressive process through which, in V. Gordon Childe's well-known phrase, "man makes himself" (p. xxiii). While the English vernacular expression "killing time" signals recreation as opposed to work, in Eliade's account, killing time becomes an ethical imperative, the truly human vocation that leads to re-creation.

The Myth of the Eternal Return exhibits, throughout, Eliade's extension of the category of "archaic" or "traditional" religion beyond the ancient Eurasian and Mesoamerican agricultural civilizations to include those peoples "usually known as 'primitive'" (p. 3), and, for that matter, contemporary "peasant masses" (p. 147) that had become a distinctive feature of his work since the mid-1930s. In the main, the Eliadean vocabulary for describing religion as an "archaic ontology" was first developed with respect to these ancient civilizations, responsive to important contemporary currents of scholarship on their texts and artifacts, and then transported to "primitive" cultures. Whether this transposition is justified remains an enduring question in evaluating Eliade's project—I think not, and Eliade occasionally distinguishes "archaic" from "primitive" in the course of this work (for example, pp. 74–75). Already in its opening chapter, *The Myth of the Eternal Return* provided most of its English-speaking readers with their initial introduction to this vocabulary, crucial to the understanding of Eliade's work, including "hierophany" (p. 4), "mythical/ideal prototypes" (pp. 4, 6), *in illo tempore* (p. 4), *ab origine* (p. 4), "repetition" (p. 5), "paradigmatic" (p. 5), "archetype" (p. 5), "the Center" (p. 5), "correspondence" (p. 6), "transformation of chaos into cosmos" (p. 10), "imitation of the Creation" (p. 11), "the sacred" (p. 11), "the real" (p. 11), *axis mundi* (p. 12), *imago mundi* (p. 17), "consecration" (p. 18), "initiation" (p. 18, cf. "the ordeal," p. 41), "cosmic regeneration" (p. 25), "desacralization" (p. 28), "profane" (pp. 27–28), "abolition of profane time, of duration, of history" (p. 35), "the regeneration of time" (p. 37). Many of these terms, ranging from "hierophany" to "sacred" (as a noun rather than an adjective), although widely used by other authors since Eliade, have yet to find a place in English-language dictionaries. The attentive reader will need to make her own lexicon as she makes her way through the book.

A second characteristic of Eliade's endeavor becomes apparent by the time the reader has progressed through the first chapter: the astonishing number of cultures passed under review (more than twenty in the first fifteen pages), represented by short quotations (the longest one, on p. 30, is eighty-eight words) drawn from works of scholarship in any one of half a dozen European languages, and largely presented without contextual details. Yet each cluster of quotations is treated as thematically related, often translated into an ontological language of "being," "reality," and the like, the result of what Eliade terms, in a paragraph added to this English translation, a process of "penetrating the authentic meaning of an archaic myth or symbol," of hearing what is being "revealed in a coherent fashion" (p. 3), without, unfortunately, in this work, clarifying how this interpretative process is undertaken and these results achieved. That is to say, it is one thing to note that, in a variety of cultures, possession of new territory is often accompanied by ritual; it may even be persuasive that these rites, if taken as a set, have as their model some imitation of divine acts of creation; but it is surely another thing to assert that these rituals of consecration "reveal the primitive's obsession with the real, his thirst for being" (p. 11).

This said, nothing should be allowed to interfere with the reader's excitement in the audacity and industry of Eliade's project, in his exercise of a synthetic imagination which forges a coherent whole out of apparently disparate items. Whether accepted as a work of science or of art, *The Myth of the Eternal Return* is a classic and founding work of what became, in the 1960s through the 1980s, a dominant mode of understanding religion, named by Eliade and others as the History of Religions.

There can be no doubt that Eliade, in chapters 1 and 2

of *The Myth of the Eternal Return,* has persuasively documented in a number of ancient civilizations the presence of
one sort of "archaic ontology"—one that conceives of the
terrestrial realm as a copy of the celestial; one that claims
that proper human praxis in all its modalities repeats the
models provided by divine activities as displayed in myths;
and that, therefore, values human creativity to the degree
that it is imitative, rather than freely original. One simply
cannot understand the great imperial cosmologies of
Eurasia and Mesoamerica, which narrate complex histories of order, without understanding this sort of "ontology" that takes as its imperative the Hermetic maxim "as
above, so below." The vast systems of correspondences developed by these literate civilizations in their texts as well
as exhibited in their large urban constructions insistently
testify to this ideology, which, above all, centers on the
cosmic responsibilities of the sacred king for maintaining
this order, for rectifying discrepancy, for subduing disor-
der. I cannot imagine any other way of interpreting a text
such as the ancient Sumerian *Creation of the Pick-axe,*
which tells of the king-god's construction of the prototyp-
ical pick-axe by means of which he separates sky from
earth and plants the seeds of humanity. The king-god uses
this tool both to enforce the distinction between heaven
and earth and to maintain the separation of the sides of
the furrow into which humankind is sown—both actions
insuring room for terrestrial growth. The text continues
with an account of human times: the Sumerian king now
uses the same sort of tool as a weapon to weed out (destroy) rebellious cities and protect loyal cities; the slave
now uses the same sort of tool as an agricultural imple-
ment to chop out weeds (understood as rebellious plants)
and to cultivate useful vegetation. All three sets of order-
ing acts are viewed as equivalent in their maintenance of

distinction, in their rejection of mixture. In principle, it would be as negligent, and, therefore, as cosmically disastrous for the slave to permit weeds to mingle with desirable plants, or for the king to tolerate rebellion, as it would be for the king-god to allow earth to reunite with sky.

Eliade, I repeat, has effectively *described* the sort of cosmopolitical worldview implicit in such a text and has given us grounds for comparing it with other texts of a similar character. In so doing, he has made both intelligible and compelling a vast assembly of religious expressions and activities. So many texts really do appear to operate by the logic he has limned out. He has been equally insistent as to their *explanation*. Eliade has made a dramatic wager that these texts may be read *without suspicion*, that one needs only to *paraphrase* them into Platonic terminology (pp. 34–35) for their "truth" to be apparent. The mundane world, the human world, takes on reality only to the degree that it participates in that which is "beyond," in that which is transmundane and transhuman. "[A]n object or an act becomes real only insofar as it imitates or repeats an archetype. Thus, reality is acquired solely through repetition or participation; everything which lacks an exemplary model is 'meaningless,' i.e., it lacks reality" (p. 34). In religious terms, this "reality" is equivalent to the sacred; "meaninglessness," to the profane.

> [T]he desire felt by the man of traditional societies to refuse history, and to confine himself to an indefinite repetition of archetypes, testifies to his thirst for the real and his terror of 'losing' himself by letting himself be overwhelmed by the meaninglessness of profane existence. . . . [His] behavior is governed by the belief in an absolute reality opposed to the profane world of 'unrealities'; in the last analysis, the latter

does not constitute a 'world,' properly speaking; it is the 'unreal' *par excellence*, the uncreated, the nonexistent: the void. (pp. 91–92)

Other explanations are possible, which may prove equally compelling. While granting the cogency of Eliade's description, these would require a measure of suspicion toward these ancient texts, as well as a willingness to translate them into a less synonymous language. One might, for example, reverse the polarities of the maxim "as above, so below," yielding the formula "as below, so above," thereby suggesting some theory of projection in the service of legitimating human institutions and practices. One might re-contextualize the chiefly Eurasian texts and traditions on which Eliade has focused by noting that they are largely documents from urban, agricultural, hierarchical civilizations, the products of well-organized scribal elites who had a deeply vested interest in structures of conformity, and in celebrating the status of the king as well as the temples on which their livelihood depended. But to do so would be to value the anthropological over the ontological, a re-valuation that Eliade refuses as a matter of principle insofar as it gives aid and comfort to the view that "man makes himself," thereby, for him, substituting a modernist view for that which is "archaic," in which human beings do not make themselves but rather are made. "[T]he archaic man acknowledges no act which has not been previously posited and lived by someone else, some other being who was not a man. What he does has been done before. His life is the ceaseless repetition of gestures initiated by others" (p. 5).

Chapter 2, which focuses more on ritual than on myth, has already laid the groundwork for what will become the theme of chapters 3 and 4: a cyclical understanding of time that, by focusing on the repetition of beginnings and endings, testifies to the belief that time periodically is halted ("abolished"), then recommenced ("regenerated"). Whether such cycles are compressed into New Year rituals, extended through vast cosmic (often lunar) cycles of creation/chaos/re-creation, or anthropologized in initiatory scenarios of death (ordeals) and rebirth, this repetitive, cyclical view is "antihistorical [in] intent," resulting in a "primitive" who "lives in a continual present" (pp. 85, 86). "[I]nterest in the 'irreversible' and the 'new' in history is a recent discovery in the life of humanity. On the contrary, archaic humanity . . . defended itself, to the utmost of its powers, against all the novelty and irreversibility which history entails" (p. 48).

Chapters 3 and 4 turn to understanding the implications of this "recent discovery in the life of humanity," and are, therefore, as explicitly reflective as they are descriptive. For this reason, "modern man" begins to intrude on Eliade's exposition, just about midway through the work (pp. 76–77), with Hegel and post-Hegelian thought—most especially "Marxism, historicism, and existentialism" (pp. xxiii and 156n)—serving as emblems of modernity and its anxieties. These become objects of Eliade's sharp critique, genealogical constructions, and cautious efforts at rehabilitation.

Eliade persistently contrasts archaic cosmic sacrality as "reality," guaranteed by the repetition of archetypes, with the "terror" of being "overwhelmed by the meaninglessness of profane existence" (p. 92), whether this "meaninglessness" be experienced as nothingness, death (annihilation), suffering, or the absurd. Whether expressed on a cosmic level as the periodic return to chaos or on the anthropological plane in the ordeals of initiation, these apparent perturbations are "fitted into a system" that guarantees that they are neither accidental nor absurd. This insures "that suffering is never final; that death is always followed by resurrection; that every defeat is annulled and transcended by the final victory" (p. 101). "[T]he important point for us is that nowhere—within the frame of the archaic civilizations—are suffering and pain regarded as 'blind' and without meaning" (p. 98). This same capacity to "fit" the vicissitudes of existence "into a system" is exhibited in the great cyclical theories of history, ranging from the Indic to the Roman, with their attendant myths of successive ages which degenerate until regenerated by a "return" (pp. 112-17).

The first important modulation of this archaic pattern occurs with the Hebrew Bible, especially with the prophets. In what, at first reading, may seem to be some of Eliade's more eccentric writing (pp. 102–12), Eliade locates himself within a scholarly and theological tradition, beginning with the late nineteenth-century Panbabylonian school, that views the Israelitic religion as breaking with the mythic, cyclical view of the ancient Near Eastern religions and introducing, in its place, a historical, lineal view of God intervening in history, of "irreversible," "one-way time" (p. 104).

[F]or the first time, we find affirmed, and increasingly accepted, the idea that historical events have a value in themselves, insofar as they are determined by the will of God. This God of the Jewish people is no longer an Oriental divinity, creator of archetypal gestures, but a personality who ceaselessly intervenes in history. . . . Historical facts thus become 'situations' of man in respect to God, and as such they acquire a religious value that nothing had previously been able to confer on them. It may, then, be said with truth that the Hebrews were the first to discover the meaning of

history as the epiphany of God, and this conception,
as we should expect, was taken up and amplified by
Christianity. (p. 104)

Likewise Abraham's willingness to sacrifice Isaac reveals
"a new religious experience, faith . . . a new religious position of man in the cosmos" (pp. 109–10, cf. pp. 160–61), no
longer a collective ritual but an individual relation. Both
the prophetic and the Abrahamic are new modalities of the
sacred insofar as they originate in revelation ("theophanies") and have as their end the "salvation" of time. Such
a worldview is different from, yet parallel to, the archaic,
especially when expressed in messianic or eschatological
myths, which look forward to the ultimate abolition of history, not by means of the archaic repetition of archetypes,
but through the imagination of a distant future. "[The]
periodic regeneration of the Creation is replaced by a single regeneration that will take place in an *in illo tempore* to
come. But the will to put a final and definitive end to history is itself still an antihistorical attitude, exactly as are
the other [archaic] traditional conceptions" (p. 112). Such
eschatologies would be further elaborated in later Chris-
tianities (pp. 143–45), as well as disguised in secular philosophies of history, such as Marxism (p. 149).

For Eliade, such a re-valuing of history as an "epiphany," as an irreversible, linear process, carries with it a
temptation, that rather than a recollection there will be a
forgetfulness of the divine; that rather than a myth of the
future abolition of time, there will be a myth of an extended future of unlimited progress undertaken by autonomous individuals; that "becoming" will be taken for
"being" as the locus of meaning—a temptation he dates as
beginning with seventeenth-century European thought (p.
145) and culminating in nineteenth- and early twentieth-

century "historicistic philosophies" (pp. 149–50)—which results in "modern man's" anxiety and "despair" in the face of the "terror of history." "[T]he man who has left the horizon of archetypes and repetition can no longer defend himself against that terror except through the idea of God" (pp. 161–62). From the perspective of "the paradise of archetypes and repetition" (see already p. 74), the faith of "modern man" in history and progress constitutes a "fall" (p. 162). It is an aberration within the general history of human kind, rather than history's culmination.

As will be clear to any reader, in this final chapter, Eliade steps forth as an odd sort of theologian, deeply ambivalent with respect to Christianity. On the one hand, "Christianity is the 'religion' of modern man and historical man, of the man who simultaneously discovered personal freedom and continuous time (in place of cyclical time). . . . Christianity incontestably proves to be the religion of 'fallen man'" (pp. 161, 162). On the other hand, there is a demythologizing tendency in Christianity that enables replication on the individual plane of elements of the older collective and cosmic renewal:

> Since what is involved is a religious experience wholly different from the traditional experience, since what is involved is faith, Christianity translates the periodic regeneration of the world into a regeneration of the human individual. But for him who shares in this eternal *nunc* of the reign of God, history ceases as totally as it does for the man of the archaic cultures, who abolishes it periodically. Consequently, for the Christian too, history can be regenerated, by and through each individual believer, even before the Saviour's second coming, when it will utterly cease for all Creation. (pp. 129–30)

This paradox of an understanding of history as being, at one and the same time, a meaningful medium of revelation, and that which needs to be overcome, a paradox which is the source of Eliade's ambivalence, is destroyed, for Eliade, when the anthropological dimension alone is affirmed at the expense of the onto-theological. To fully understand Eliade at this point, it would be necessary to go beyond this book, to his further articulations of these themes, and to a fuller understanding of the Orthodox Christian tradition out of which he writes.

The Myth of the Eternal Return is not itself a timeless work. It is clearly located in a wider cultural milieu following immediately upon the end of World War II and the beginning of the Cold War. One cannot miss the engagement with contemporary thinkers, "[o]nly the historicistic position, in all its varieties and shades—from Nietzsche's 'destiny' to Heidegger's 'temporality'—remains disarmed [before the 'terror of history']" (p. 152), or his references to contemporary literature (p. 153). Even more, one cannot miss the concreteness of his references to contemporary "horrors of history":

[W]e are concerned with the problem of history as history, of the 'evil' that is bound up not with man's condition but with his behavior toward others. We should wish to know, for example, how it would be possible to tolerate, and to justify, the sufferings and annihilation of so many peoples who suffer and are annihilated for the simple reason that their geographical situation sets them in the pathway of history; that they are neighbors of empires in a state of permanent expansion.... And in our day, when historical pressure no longer allows any escape, how can man tolerate the catastrophes and horrors of history—from

collective deportations and massacres to atomic bombings? (p. 151)

Eliade, in this work, offers not so much a remedy as a di-
agnosis of the consequences of the modernist view that
limits the anthropological horizon to "'historical man' . . .
the man who *is* insofar as he *makes himself, within history*"
(p. xxiii). Unlike other traditionist thinkers, with whom he
is sometimes associated, Eliade knows that a "return" to
(let alone a conversion to) archaic religion is not possible
for modern man, even though elements of the former may
persist in modernity, often in "disguised" or "unconscious"
forms. In his foreword he sets forth a more modest goal,
"to draw the attention of the philosopher, and of the cultivated man in general, to certain spiritual positions that, although they have been transcended in various regions of
the globe, are instructive" (p. xxv). While, in other writings contemporary with *The Myth of the Eternal Return*,
Eliade advocated the value of a "meeting," an "encounter,"
a "confrontation," between the archaic worldview and ours,
now that contemporary representatives of the archaic have
entered into *our* history, in this book, most especially in
the opening chapters, it is the descriptive endeavor that
prevails, with the reader tacitly invited to enter into a dialogue with the thought of others for too long placed at the
level of childish "primitives" or idolatrous "heathens" in
histories of progress. As I have suggested above, it is these
same descriptive chapters that have stood the test of time.

FOREWORD

HAD WE not feared to appear overambitious, we should have given this book a subtitle: *Introduction to a Philosophy of History*. For such, after all, is the purport of the present essay; but with the distinction that, instead of proceeding to a speculative analysis of the historical phenomenon, it examines the fundamental concepts of archaic societies—societies which, although they are conscious of a certain form of "history," make every effort to disregard it. In studying these traditional societies, one characteristic has especially struck us: it is their revolt against concrete, historical time, their nostalgia for a periodical return to the mythical time of the beginning of things, to the "Great Time." The meaning and function of what we have called "archetypes and repetition" disclosed themselves to us only after we had perceived these societies' will to refuse concrete time, their hostility toward every attempt at autonomous "history," that is, at history not regulated by archetypes. This dismissal, this opposition, are not merely the effect of the conservative tendencies of primitive societies, as this book proves. In our opinion, it is justifiable to read in this depreciation of history (that is, of events without transhistorical models), and in this rejection of profane, continuous time, a certain metaphysical "valorization" of human existence. But this valorization is emphatically not that which certain post-Hegelian philosophical currents—notably Marxism, historicism, and existentialism—have sought to give to it since the discovery of "historical man," of the man who *is* insofar as he *makes himself, within history*.

The problem of history as history, however, will not be directly approached in this essay. Our chief intent has been to set forth certain governing lines of force in the speculative field of archaic societies. It seemed to us that a simple presentation of this field would not be without interest, especially for the philosopher accustomed to finding his problems and the means of solving them in the texts of classic philosophy or in the situations of the spiritual history of the West. With us, it is an old conviction that Western philosophy is dangerously close to "provincializing" itself (if the expression be permitted): first by jealously isolating itself in its own tradition and ignoring, for example, the problems and solutions of Oriental thought; second by its obstinate refusal to recognize any "situations" except those of the man of the historical civilizations, in defiance of the experience of "primitive" man, of man as a member of the traditional societies. We hold that philosophical anthropology would have something to learn from the valorization that pre-Socratic man (in other words, traditional man) accorded to his situation in the universe. Better yet: that the cardinal problems of metaphysics could be renewed through a knowledge of archaic ontology. In several previous works, especially in our *Patterns in Comparative Religion*, we attempted to present the principles of this archaic ontology, without claiming, of course, to have succeeded in giving a coherent, still less an exhaustive, exposition of it.

This study, likewise, does not attempt to be exhaustive. Addressing ourselves both to the philosopher and to the ethnologist or orientalist, but above all to the cultivated man, to the nonspecialist, we have often compressed into brief statements what, if duly investigated and differentiated, would demand a substantial book. Any thoroughgoing discussion would have entailed a marshaling of sources and a technical language that would have discouraged many readers. But instead of furnishing specialists with a series of marginal comments upon their particular problems, our concern has been to draw the attention of the philosopher, and of the cultivated man in general, to certain spiritual positions that, although they have been transcended in various regions of the globe, are instructive for our knowledge of man and for man's history itself.

*

This essay appeared in French in 1949 as *Le Mythe de l'éternel retour: archétypes et répétition* (Paris, Librairie Gallimard). On the occasion of the present English translation we have revised and enlarged the text and have included in the footnotes references to certain studies published within the last few years.

Paris, October, 1952

*

For the second printing, aside from minor corrections in the text, the bibliography and footnotes have been revised in order to include subsequent translations of my works and some others.

Chicago, June, 1965   M. E.

PREFACE*

THE manuscript that I began in May, 1945, was headed *Cosmos and History*. It was only later that I changed its title to *Archetypes and Repetition*. But finally, at the suggestion of the French publisher, I made *Archetypes and Repetition* the subtitle, and the book was published in 1949 as *The Myth of the Eternal Return* (*Le Mythe de l'éternel retour*). This has sometimes given rise to misunderstandings. For one thing, the archaic ideology of ritual repetition, which was the central subject of my study, does not always imply the "myth of the eternal return." And then too, such a title could lead the reader to suppose that the book was principally concerned with the celebrated Greek myth or with its modern reinterpretation by Nietzsche, which is by no means the case.

The essential theme of my investigation bears on the image of himself formed by the man of the archaic societies and on the place that he assumes in the Cosmos. The chief difference between the man of the archaic and traditional societies and the man of the modern societies with their strong imprint of Judaeo-Christianity lies in the fact that the former feels himself indissolubly connected with the Cosmos and the cosmic rhythms, whereas the latter insists that he is connected only

* When the present work was published in a Harper Torchbooks paperback edition in 1959, the author consented to change its title to *Cosmos and History* and prepared a special preface. The Princeton/Bollingen paperback edition, with Professor Eliade's permission, restored the original English title. The 1959 preface is given here, with the omission of its opening and closing phrases. The text of the book is that of the corrected second printing of 1965, including the complete bibliography.—EDITOR.

with History. Of course, for the man of the archaic societies, the Cosmos too has a "history," if only because it is the creation of the gods and is held to have been organized by supernatural beings or mythical heroes. But this "history" of the Cosmos and of human society is a "sacred history," preserved and transmitted through myths. More than that, it is a "history" that can be repeated indefinitely, in the sense that the myths serve as models for ceremonies that periodically reactualize the tremendous events that occurred at the beginning of time. The myths preserve and transmit the paradigms, the exemplary models, for all the responsible activities in which men engage. By virtue of these paradigmatic models revealed to men in mythical times, the Cosmos and society are periodically regenerated. Later on in this book I discuss the effects that this faithful reproduction of paradigms and this ritual repetition of mythical events will have on the religious ideology of the archaic peoples. It is not difficult to understand why such an ideology makes it impossible that what we today call a "historical consciousness" should develop.

In the course of the book I have used the terms "exemplary models," "paradigms," and "archetypes" in order to emphasize a particular fact—namely, that for the man of the traditional and archaic societies, the models for his institutions and the norms for his various categories of behavior are believed to have been "revealed" at the beginning of time, that, consequently, they are regarded as having a superhuman and "transcendental" origin. In using the term "archetype," I neglected to specify that I was not referring to the archetypes described by Professor C. G. Jung. This was a regrettable error. For to use, in an entirely different meaning, a term that plays a role of primary importance in Jung's psychology could lead to confusion. I need scarcely say that, for Professor Jung, the archetypes are structures of the collective unconscious. But in my book I nowhere touch upon the problems of depth psychology nor do I use the concept of the collective unconscious. As I have said, I use the term "archetype," just as Eugenio d'Ors does, as a synonym for "exemplary model" or "paradigm," that is, in the last analysis, in the Augustinian sense. But in our day the word has been rehabilitated by Professor Jung, who has given it a new meaning; and it is certainly desirable that the term "archetype" should no longer be used in its pre-Jungian sense unless the fact is distinctly stated.

An author is seldom satisfied with his work ten years after finishing it. There is no doubt that, if I were writing this little book now, it would be very different. Yet such as it is, with all its faults of commission and omission, I still consider it the most significant of my books; and when I am asked in what order they should be read, I always recommend beginning with the present work.

MIRCEA ELIADE

University of Chicago
November, 1958

CHAPTER ONE

ARCHETYPES AND REPETITION

*The Problem · Celestial Archetypes of
Territories, Temples, and Cities · The Symbolism of the
Center · Repetition of the Cosmogony · Divine
Models of Rituals · Archetypes of Profane
Activities · Myths and History*

*

The Problem

THIS book undertakes to study certain aspects of archaic ontology—more precisely, the conceptions of being and reality that can be read from the behavior of the man of the premodern societies. The premodern or "traditional" societies include both the world usually known as "primitive" and the ancient cultures of Asia, Europe, and America. Obviously, the metaphysical concepts of the archaic world were not always formulated in theoretical language; but the symbol, the myth, the rite, express, on different planes and through the means proper to them, a complex system of coherent affirmations about the ultimate reality of things, a system that can be regarded as constituting a metaphysics. It is, however, essential to understand the deep meaning of all these symbols, myths, and rites, in order to succeed in translating them into our habitual language. If one goes to the trouble of penetrating the authentic meaning of an archaic myth or symbol, one cannot but observe that this meaning shows a recognition of a certain situation in the cosmos and that, consequently, it implies a metaphysical position. It is useless to search archaic languages for the terms so laboriously created by the great philosophical traditions: there is every likelihood that such words as "being," "nonbeing," "real," "unreal," "becoming," "illusory," are not to be found in the language of the Australians or of the ancient Mesopotamians. But if the word is lacking, the *thing* is present; only it is "said"—that is, revealed in a coherent fashion—through symbols and myths.

If we observe the general behavior of archaic man, we are struck by the following fact: neither the objects of the external world nor human acts, properly speaking, have any autonomous intrinsic value. Objects or acts acquire a

value, and in so doing become real, because they participate, after one fashion or another, in a reality that tran-
scends them. Among countless stones, one stone becomes
sacred—and hence instantly becomes saturated with being
—because it constitutes a hierophany, or possesses mana,
or again because it commemorates a mythical act, and so
on. The object appears as the receptacle of an exterior
force that differentiates it from its milieu and gives it
meaning and value. This force may reside in the substance
of the object or in its form; a rock reveals itself to be
sacred because its very existence is a hierophany: incom-
pressible, invulnerable, it is that which man is not. It re-
sists time; its reality is coupled with perenniality. Take
the commonest of stones; it will be raised to the rank of
"precious," that is, impregnated with a magical or religious power by virtue of its symbolic shape or its origin:
thunderstone, held to have fallen from the sky; pearl, because it comes from the depths of the sea. Other stones
will be sacred because they are the dwelling place of the
souls of ancestors (India, Indonesia), or because they were
once the scene of a theophany (as the *bethel* that served
Jacob for a bed), or because a sacrifice or an oath has consecrated them.[1]

Now let us turn to human acts—those, of course, which
do not arise from pure automatism. Their meaning, their
value, are not connected with their crude physical datum
but with their property of reproducing a primordial act, of
repeating a mythical example. Nutrition is not a simple
physiological operation; it renews a communion. Marriage
and the collective orgy echo mythical prototypes; they are
repeated because they were consecrated in the beginning
("in those days," *in illo tempore, ab origine*) by gods, ancestors, or heroes.

[1] Cf. our *Patterns in Comparative Religion* (English trans., London and New
York, 1958), pp. 216 ff.

4

In the particulars of his conscious behavior, the "primitive," the archaic man, acknowledges no act which has not been previously posited and lived by someone else, some other being who was not a man. What he does has been done before. His life is the ceaseless repetition of gestures initiated by others.

This conscious repetition of given paradigmatic gestures reveals an original ontology. The crude product of nature, the object fashioned by the industry of man, acquire their reality, their identity, only to the extent of their participation in a transcendent reality. The gesture acquires meaning, reality, solely to the extent to which it repeats a primordial act.

Various groups of facts, drawn here and there from different cultures, will help us to identify the structure of this archaic ontology. We have first sought out examples likely to show, as clearly as possible, the mechanism of traditional thought; in other words, facts which help us to understand how and why, for the man of the premodern societies, certain things become real.

It is essential to understand this mechanism thoroughly, in order that we may afterward approach the problem of human existence and of history within the horizon of archaic spirituality.

We have distributed our collection of facts under several principal headings:

1. Facts which show us that, for archaic man, reality is a function of the imitation of a celestial archetype.

2. Facts which show us how reality is conferred through participation in the "symbolism of the Center": cities, temples, houses become real by the fact of being assimilated to the "center of the world."

3. Finally, rituals and significant profane gestures which acquire the meaning attributed to them, and materialize that meaning, only because they deliberately repeat such

and such acts posited *ab origine* by gods, heroes, or ancestors.

The presentation of these facts will in itself lay the groundwork for a study and interpretation of the ontological conception underlying them.

Celestial Archetypes of Territories, Temples, and Cities

ACCORDING to Mesopotamian beliefs, the Tigris has its model in the star Anunit and the Euphrates in the star of the Swallow.[2] A Sumerian text tells of the "place of the creation of the gods," where "the [divinity of] the flocks and grains" is to be found.[3] For the Ural-Altaic peoples the mountains, in the same way, have an ideal prototype in the sky.[4] In Egypt, places and nomes were named after the celestial "fields": first the celestial fields were known, then they were identified in terrestrial geography.[5]

In Iranian cosmology of the Zarvanitic tradition, "every terrestrial phenomenon, whether abstract or concrete, corresponds to a celestial, transcendent invisible term, to an "idea" in the Platonic sense. Each thing, each notion presents itself under a double aspect: that of *mēnōk* and that of *gētīk*. There is a visible sky: hence there is also a *mēnōk* sky which is invisible (*Bundahišn*, Ch. I). Our earth corresponds to a celestial earth. Each virtue practiced here below, in the *gētāh*, has a celestial counterpart which represents true reality. . . . The year, prayer . . . in short, whatever is manifested in the *gētāh*, is at the same time

[2] Our *Cosmologie şi alchimie babiloniană* (Bucharest, 1937), pp. 21 ff.
[3] Edward Chiera, *Sumerian Religious Texts*, I (Upland, 1924), p. 29.
[4] Uno Harva (formerly Holmberg), *Der Baum des Lebens* (Annales Accademiae Scientiarum Fennicae, Helsinki, 1923), p. 39.
[5] Raymond Weill, *Le Champs des roseaux et le champs des offrandes dans la religion funéraire et la religion générale* (Paris, 1936), pp. 62 ff.

mēnōk. The creation is simply duplicated. From the cosmogonic point of view the cosmic stage called *mēnōk* precedes the stage *gētīk*." [6]

The temple in particular—pre-eminently the sacred place—had a celestial prototype. On Mount Sinai, Jehovah shows Moses the "form" of the sanctuary that he is to build for him: "According to all that I shew thee, after the pattern of the tabernacle, and the pattern of all the instruments thereof, even so shall ye make it. . . . And look that thou make them after their pattern, which was shewed thee in the mount" (Exodus 25 : 9, 40). And when David gives his son Solomon the plan for the temple buildings, for the tabernacle, and for all their utensils, he assures him that "All this . . . the Lord made me understand in writing by his hand upon me, even all the works of this pattern" (I Chronicles 28 : 19). Hence he had seen the celestial model.[7]

The earliest document referring to the archetype of a sanctuary is Gudea's inscription concerning the temple he built at Lagash. In a dream the king sees the goddess Nidaba, who shows him a tablet on which the beneficent stars are named, and a god who reveals the plan of the temple to him.[8] Cities too have their divine prototypes. All the Babylonian cities had their archetypes in the con-

[6] H. S. Nyberg, "Questions de cosmogonie et de cosmologie mazdéennes," *Journal Asiatique* (Paris), CCXIX (July–Sept., 1931), pp. 35–36. But, as Henry Corbin rightly remarks, "we must take care not to reduce the contrast they [the *mēnōk* and the *gētīk*] express to a Platonic schema pure and simple. We are not dealing precisely with an opposition between idea and matter, or between the universal and the perceptible. *Mēnōk* should, rather, be translated by a celestial, invisible, spiritual, but perfectly concrete state. *Gētīk* designates an earthly visible, material state, but of a matter which is in itself wholly luminous, a matter immaterial in relation to the matter that we actually know." Corbin, "Cyclical Time in Mazdaism and Ismailism," in *Man and Time* (New York and London, 1957), p. 118.

[7] Cf. the rabbinical traditions in Raphael Patai, *Man and Temple* (London, 1947), pp. 130 ff.

[8] E. Burrows, "Some Cosmological Patterns in Babylonian Religion," in *The Labyrinth*, ed. S. H. Hooke (London, 1935), pp. 65 ff.

stellations: Sippara in Cancer, Nineveh in Ursa Major, Assur in Arcturus, etc.[9] Sennacherib has Nineveh built according to the "form . . . delineated from distant ages by the writing of the heaven-of-stars." Not only does a model precede terrestrial architecture, but the model is also situated in an ideal (celestial) region of eternity. This is what Solomon announces: "Thou gavest command to build a sanctuary in thy holy mountain, And an altar in the city of thy habitation, A copy of the holy tabernacle which thou preparedst aforehand from the beginning." [10]

A celestial Jerusalem was created by God before the city was built by the hand of man; it is to the former that the prophet refers in the Syriac Apocalypse of Baruch II, 4 : 2-7: " 'Dost thou think that this is that city of which I said: "On the palms of My hands have I graven thee"? This building now built in your midst is not that which is revealed with Me, that which was prepared beforehand here from the time when I took counsel to make Paradise, and showed it to Adam before he sinned . . .' " [11] The heavenly Jerusalem kindled the inspiration of all the Hebrew prophets: Tobias 13 : 16; Isaiah 59 : 11 ff.; Ezekiel 60, etc. To show him the city of Jerusalem, God lays hold of Ezekiel in an ecstatic vision and transports him to a very high mountain. And the *Sibylline Oracles* preserve the memory of the New Jerusalem in the center of which there shines "a temple . . . with a giant tower touching the very clouds and seen of all . . ." [12] But the most beautiful description of the heavenly Jerusalem occurs in the Apoc-

---

[9] Cf. our *Cosmologie*, p. 22; Burrows, pp. 60 ff.

[10] Wisdom of Solomon 9 : 8; trans. in R. H. Charles, *The Apocrypha and Pseudepigrapha of the Old Testament in English* (Oxford, 1913), I, p. 549.

[11] Charles, II, p. 482.

[12] Charles, II, p. 405; Alberto Pincherle, *Gli Oracoli Sibillini giudaici* (Rome, 1922), pp. 95-96.

alypse (21 : 2 ff.): "And I John saw the holy city, new Jerusalem, coming down from God out of heaven, prepared as a bride adorned for her husband."

We find the same theory in India: all the Indian royal cities, even the modern ones, are built after the mythical model of the celestial city where, in the age of gold (*in illo tempore*), the Universal Sovereign dwelt. And, like the latter, the king attempts to revive the age of gold, to make a perfect reign a present reality—an idea which we shall encounter again in the course of this study. Thus, for example, the palace-fortress of Sigiriya, in Ceylon, is built after the model of the celestial city Alakamanda and is "hard of ascent for human beings" (*Mahāvastu*, 39, 2). Plato's ideal city likewise has a celestial archetype (*Republic*, 592b; cf. 500e). The Platonic "forms" are not astral; yet their mythical region is situated on supraterrestrial planes (*Phaedrus*, 247, 250).

The world that surrounds us, then, the world in which the presence and the work of man are felt—the mountains that he climbs, populated and cultivated regions, navigable rivers, cities, sanctuaries—all these have an extraterrestrial archetype, be it conceived as a plan, as a form, or purely and simply as a "double" existing on a higher cosmic level. But everything in the world that surrounds us does not have a prototype of this kind. For example, desert regions inhabited by monsters, uncultivated lands, unknown seas on which no navigator has dared to venture, do not share with the city of Babylon, or the Egyptian nome, the privilege of a differentiated prototype. They correspond to a mythical model, but of another nature: all these wild, uncultivated regions and the like are assimilated to chaos; they still participate in the undifferentiated, formless modality of pre-Creation. This is why, when posses-

9

sion is taken of a territory—that is, when its exploitation begins—rites are performed that symbolically repeat the act of Creation: the uncultivated zone is first "cosmicized," then inhabited. We shall presently return to the meaning of this ceremonial taking possession of newly discovered countries. For the moment, what we wish to emphasize is the fact that the world which surrounds us, civilized by the hand of man, is accorded no validity beyond that which is due to the extraterrestrial prototype that served as its model. Man constructs according to an archetype. Not only do his city or his temple have celestial models; the same is true of the entire region that he inhabits, with the rivers that water it, the fields that give him his food, etc. The map of Babylon shows the city at the center of a vast circular territory bordered by a river, precisely as the Sumerians envisioned Paradise. This participation by urban cultures in an archetypal model is what gives them their reality and their validity.

Settlement in a new, unknown, uncultivated country is equivalent to an act of Creation. When the Scandinavian colonists took possession of Iceland, *Landnáma*, and began to cultivate it, they regarded this act neither as an original undertaking nor as human and profane work. Their enterprise was for them only the repetition of a primordial act: the transformation of chaos into cosmos by the divine act of Creation. By cultivating the desert soil, they in fact repeated the act of the gods, who organized chaos by giving it forms and norms.[13] Better still, a territorial conquest does not become real until after—more precisely, through —the ritual of taking possession, which is only a copy of the primordial act of the Creation of the World. In Vedic India the erection of an altar dedicated to Agni

---

[13] Cf. van Hamel, cited by Gerardus van der Leeuw, *L'Homme primitif et la religion* (French trans., Paris, 1940), p. 110.

constituted legal taking possession of a territory.[14] "One settles (*avasyati*) when he builds the *gārhapatya*, and whoever are builders of fire-altars are 'settled' (*avasitāḥ*)," says the *Śatapatha Brāhmaṇa* (VII, 1, 1, 1–4). But the erection of an altar dedicated to Agni is merely the microcosmic imitation of the Creation. Furthermore, any sacrifice is, in turn, the repetition of the act of Creation, as Indian texts explicitly state.[15] It was in the name of Jesus Christ that the Spanish and Portuguese conquistadores took possession of the islands and continents that they had discovered and conquered. The setting up of the Cross was equivalent to a justification and to the consecration of the new country, to a "new birth," thus repeating baptism (act of Creation). In their turn the English navigators took possession of conquered countries in the name of the king of England, new Cosmocrator.

The importance of the Vedic, Scandinavian, or Roman ceremonials will appear more clearly when we devote a separate examination to the meaning of the repetition of the Creation, the pre-eminently divine act. For the moment, let us keep one fact in view: every territory occupied for the purpose of being inhabited or utilized as *Lebensraum* is first of all transformed from chaos into cosmos; that is, through the effect of ritual it is given a "form" which makes it become real. Evidently, for the archaic mentality, reality manifests itself as force, effectiveness, and duration. Hence the outstanding reality is the sacred; for only the sacred *is* in an absolute fashion, acts effectively, creates things and makes them endure. The innumerable gestures of consecration—of tracts and territories, of objects, of men, etc.—reveal the primitive's obsession with the real, his thirst for being.

[14] Ananda K. Coomaraswamy, *The Ṛg Veda as Land-náma-bók* (London, 1935), p. 16, etc.
[15] For example, *Śatapatha Brāhmaṇa*, XIV, 1, 2, 26, etc.; see below, Ch. II.

The Symbolism of the Center

PARALLELING the archaic belief in the celestial archetypes of cities and temples, and even more fully attested by documents, there is, we find, another series of beliefs, which refer to their being invested with the prestige of the Center. We examined this problem in an earlier work;[16] here we shall merely recapitulate our conclusions. The architectonic symbolism of the Center may be formulated as follows:

1. The Sacred Mountain—where heaven and earth meet—is situated at the center of the world.

2. Every temple or palace—and, by extension, every sacred city or royal residence—is a Sacred Mountain, thus becoming a Center.

3. Being an *axis mundi*, the sacred city or temple is regarded as the meeting point of heaven, earth, and hell.

A few examples will illustrate each of these symbols:

1. According to Indian beliefs, Mount Meru rises at the center of the world, and above it shines the polestar. The Ural-Altaic peoples also know of a central mountain, Sumeru, to whose summit the polestar is fixed. Iranian beliefs hold that the sacred mountain Haraberezaiti (Elburz) is situated at the center of the earth and is linked with heaven.[17] The Buddhist population of Laos, north of Siam, know of Mount Zinnalo, at the center of the world. In the *Edda*, Himinbjorg, as its name indicates, is a "celestial mountain"; it is here that the rainbow (Bifrost) reaches the dome of the sky. Similar beliefs are found among the

[16] See our *Cosmologie*, pp. 26–50; cf. also our *Images and Symbols: Studies in Religious Symbolism* (English trans., London and New York, 1961), Ch. I.

[17] Willibald Kirfel, *Die Kosmographie der Inder* (Bonn, 1920), p. 15; Harva, p. 41; Arthur Christensen, *Les Types du premier homme et du premier roi dans l'histoire légendaire des Iraniens*, II (Stockholm, 1917), p. 42; our *Shamanism: Archaic Techniques of Ecstasy* (English trans., New York and London, 1964), pp. 259 ff.

Finns, the Japanese, and other peoples. We are reminded that for the Semangs of the Malay Peninsula an immense rock, Batu-Ribn, rises at the center of the world; above it is hell. In past times, a tree trunk on Batu-Ribn rose into the sky.[18] Hell, the center of the earth, and the "gate" of the sky are, then, situated on the same axis, and it is along this axis that passage from one cosmic region to another was effected. We should hesitate to credit the authenticity of this cosmological theory among the Semang pygmies if we did not have evidence that the same theory already existed in outline during the prehistoric period.[19] According to Mesopotamian beliefs, a central mountain joins heaven and earth; it is the Mount of the Lands,[20] the connection between territories. Properly speaking, the ziggurat was a cosmic mountain, i.e., a symbolic image of the cosmos, the seven stories representing the seven planetary heavens (as at Borsippa) or having the colors of the world (as at Ur).

Mount Tabor, in Palestine, could mean *ṭabbūr*, i.e., navel, *omphalos*. Mount Gerizim, in the center of Palestine, was undoubtedly invested with the prestige of the Center, for it is called "navel of the earth" (*ṭabbūr ereṣ;* cf. Judges 9 : 37: ". . . See there come people down by the middle [Heb., navel] of the land . . ."). A tradition preserved by Peter Comestor relates that at the summer solstice the sun casts no shadow on the "Fountain of Jacob" (near Gerizim). And indeed, Peter continues, "sunt qui dicunt locum illum esse umbilicum terrae nostrae habitabilis." Palestine, being the highest country—because it was near

---

[18] Cf. Paul Schebesta, *Les Pygmées* (French trans., Paris, 1940), pp. 156 ff.; other examples in our *Shamanism*, pp. 280 ff.

[19] Cf., for example, W. Gaerte, "Kosmische Vorstellungen im Bilde prähistorischer Zeit: Erdberg, Himmelsberg, Erdnabel und Weltströme," *Anthropos* (Salzburg), IX (1914), pp. 956–79.

[20] Alfred Jeremias, *Handbuch der altorientalischen Geisteskultur* (2nd edn., Berlin and Leipzig, 1929), p. 130.

to the summit of the cosmic mountain—was not covered by the Deluge. A rabbinic text says: "The land of Israel was not submerged by the deluge." [21] For Christians, Golgotha was situated at the center of the world, since it was the summit of the cosmic mountain and at the same time the place where Adam had been created and buried. Thus the blood of the Saviour falls upon Adam's skull, buried precisely at the foot of the Cross, and redeems him. The belief that Golgotha is situated at the center of the world is preserved in the folklore of the Eastern Christians.[22]

2. The names of the Babylonian temples and sacred towers themselves testify to their assimilation to the cosmic mountain: "Mount of the House," "House of the Mount of All Lands," "Mount of Tempests," "Link Between Heaven and Earth." [23] A cylinder from the period of King Gudea says that "The bed-chamber [of the god] which he built was [like] the cosmic mountain . . ." [24] Every Oriental city was situated at the center of the world. Babylon was a *Bāb-ilāni*, a "gate of the gods," for it was there that the gods descended to earth. In the capital of the Chinese sovereign, the gnomon must cast no shadow at noon on the day of the summer solstice. Such a capital is, in effect, at the center of the universe, close to the miraculous tree (*kien-mu*), at the meeting place of the three cosmic zones: heaven, earth, and hell.[25] The Javanese

[21] Cf. Burrows, pp. 51, 54, 62, note 1; A. J. Wensinck, *The Ideas of the Western Semites Concerning the Navel of the Earth* (Amsterdam, 1916), p. 15; Patai, p. 85. The same symbolism in Egypt: cf. Patai, p. 101, note 100.

[22] E.g., among the Little Russians; Mansikka, cited by Harva, p. 72.

[23] Theodor Dombart, *Der Sakralturm*, Part I: *Zikkurrat* (Munich, 1920), p. 34; cf. A. Parrot, *Ziggurats et Tour de Babel* (Paris, 1949). Indian temples are also assimilated to mountains: cf. Willy Foy, "Indische Kultbauten als Symbole des Götterbergs," in *Festschrift Ernst Windisch zum siebzigsten Geburtstag . . . Dargebracht* (Leipzig, 1914), pp. 213–16. The same symbolism among the Aztecs: cf. Walter Krickeberg, "Bauform und Weltbild im alten Mexico," *Paideuma* (Bamberg), IV (1950), 295–333.

[24] W. F. Albright, "The Mouth of the Rivers," *The American Journal of Semitic Languages and Literatures* (Chicago), XXXV (1919), p. 173.

[25] Marcel Granet, *La Pensée chinoise* (Paris, 1934), p. 324; our *Le Chamanisme*, pp. 243 ff.

temple of Borobudur is itself an image of the cosmos, and is built like an artificial mountain (as were the ziggurats). Ascending it, the pilgrim approaches the center of the world, and, on the highest terrace, breaks from one plane to another, transcending profane, heterogeneous space and entering a "pure region." Cities and sacred places are assimilated to the summits of cosmic mountains. This is why Jerusalem and Zion were not submerged by the Deluge. According to Islamic tradition, the highest point on earth is the Kaaba, because "the polestar proves that . . . it lies over against the center of heaven." [26]

3. Finally, because of its situation at the center of the cosmos, the temple or the sacred city is always the meeting point of the three cosmic regions: heaven, earth, and hell. *Dur-an-ki*, "Bond of Heaven and Earth," was the name given to the sanctuaries of Nippur and Larsa, and doubtless to that of Sippara. Babylon had many names, among them "House of the Base of Heaven and Earth," "Bond of Heaven and Earth." But it is always Babylon that is the scene of the connection between the earth and the lower regions, for the city had been built upon *bāb apsî*, the "Gate of the Apsu" [27]—*apsu* designating the waters of chaos before the Creation. We find the same tradition among the Hebrews. The rock of Jerusalem reached deep into the subterranean waters (*tehôm*). The Mishnah says that the Temple is situated exactly above the *tehôm* (Hebrew equivalent of *apsu*). And just as in Babylon there was the "gate of the *apsu*," the rock of the Temple in Jerusalem contained the "mouth of the *tehôm*." [28] We find similar conceptions in the Indo-European world. Among the Romans, for example, the *mundus*—that is, the trench dug around the place where a city was to be founded—constitutes the point where the lower regions and the terrestrial

[26] *Kisâ'î*, fol. 15; cited by Wensinck, p. 15.
[27] Jeremias, p. 113; Burrows, pp. 46 ff., 50.
[28] Texts in Burrows, p. 49; cf. also Patai, pp. 55 ff.

world meet. "When the *mundus* is open it is as if the gates of the gloomy infernal gods were open," says Varro (cited by Macrobius, *Saturnalia*, I, 16, 18). The Italic temple was the zone where the upper (divine), terrestrial, and subterranean worlds intersected.

The summit of the cosmic mountain is not only the highest point of the earth; it is also the earth's navel, the point at which the Creation began. There are even instances in which cosmological traditions explain the symbolism of the Center in terms which might well have been borrowed from embryology. "The Holy One created the world like an embryo. As the embryo proceeds from the navel onwards, so God began to create the world from its navel onwards and from there it was spread out in different directions." The *Yoma* affirms: "The world has been created beginning from Zion." [29] In the *Ṛg-Veda* (for example X, 149), the universe is conceived as spreading from a central point.[30] The creation of man, which answers to the cosmogony, likewise took place at a central point, at the center of the world. According to Mesopotamian tradition, man was formed at the "navel of the earth" in *uzu* (flesh), *sar* (bond), *ki* (place, earth), where *Dur-an-ki*, the "Bond of Heaven and Earth," is also situated. Ormazd creates the primordial ox Evagdāth, and the primordial man, Gajōmard, at the center of the earth.[31] Paradise, where Adam was created from clay, is, of course, situated at the center of the cosmos. Paradise was the navel of the Earth and, according to a Syrian tradition, was established on a mountain higher than all others. According to the Syrian *Book of the Cave of Treasures*, Adam was created at the

[29] Texts cited by Wensinck, pp. 19, 16; cf. also W. H. Roscher, "Neue Omphalosstudien," *Abhandlungen der Königlich Sächsischen Gesellschaft der Wissenschaft* (Leipzig), *Phil.-hist. Klasse*, XXXI, 1 (1915), pp. 16 ff., 73 ff.; Burrows, p. 57; Patai, p. 85.

[30] Cf. the commentary of Kirfel, p. 8.

[31] Burrows, p. 49; Christensen, I, pp. 22 ff.

center of the earth, at the same spot where the Cross of Christ was later to be set up. The same traditions have been preserved by Judaism. The Jewish apocalypse and a midrash state that Adam was formed in Jerusalem.[32] Adam being buried at the very spot where he was created, i.e., at the center of the world, on Golgotha, the blood of the Saviour—as we have seen—will redeem him too.

The symbolism of the Center is considerably more complex, but the few aspects to which we have referred will suffice for our purpose. We may add that the same symbolism survived in the Western world down to the threshold of modern times. The very ancient conception of the temple as the *imago mundi*, the idea that the sanctuary reproduces the universe in its essence, passed into the religious architecture of Christian Europe: the basilica of the first centuries of our era, like the medieval cathedral, symbolically reproduces the Celestial Jerusalem.[33] As to the symbolism of the mountain, of the Ascension, and of the "Quest for the Center," they are clearly attested in medieval literature, and appear, though only by allusion, in certain literary works of recent centuries.[34]

Repetition of the Cosmogony

THE CENTER, then, is pre-eminently the zone of the sacred, the zone of absolute reality. Similarly, all the other symbols of absolute reality (trees of life and immortality,

[32] Wensinck, p. 14; Sir E. A. Wallis Budge, *The Book of the Cave of Treasures* (trans. from the Syriac, London, 1927), p. 53; Oskar Daehnhardt, *Natursagen*, I (Leipzig, 1909), p. 112; Burrows, p. 57.

[33] On the cosmic symbolism of temples in the ancient East, cf. A. M. Hocart, *Kings and Councillors* (Cairo, 1936), pp. 220 ff.; Patai, pp. 106 ff. On the cosmic symbolism of basilicas and cathedrals, see Hans Sedlmayr, "Architectur als abbildende Kunst," *Österreichische Akademie der Wissenschaften, Sitzungsberichte* (Vienna), *Phil.-hist. Klasse*, 225/3 (1948), and *Die Kathedrale* (Zurich, 1950).

[34] See our *Images and Symbols*.

17

Fountain of Youth, etc.) are also situated at a center. The road leading to the center is a "difficult road" (*dūrohaṇa*), and this is verified at every level of reality: difficult convolutions of a temple (as at Borobudur); pilgrimage to sacred places (Mecca, Hardwar, Jerusalem); danger-ridden voyages of the heroic expeditions in search of the Golden Fleece, the Golden Apples, the Herb of Life; wanderings in labyrinths; difficulties of the seeker for the road to the self, to the "center" of his being, and so on. The road is arduous, fraught with perils, because it is, in fact, a rite of the passage from the profane to the sacred, from the ephemeral and illusory to reality and eternity, from death to life, from man to the divinity. Attaining the center is equivalent to a consecration, an initiation; yesterday's profane and illusory existence gives place to a new, to a life that is real, enduring, and effective.

If the act of the Creation realizes the passage from the nonmanifest to the manifest or, to speak cosmologically, from chaos to cosmos; if the Creation took place from a center; if, consequently, all the varieties of being, from the inanimate to the living, can attain existence only in an area dominantly sacred—all this beautifully illuminates for us the symbolism of sacred cities (centers of the world), the geomantic theories that govern the foundation of towns, the conceptions that justify the rites accompanying their building. We studied these construction rites, and the theories which they imply, in an earlier work,[35] and to this we refer the reader. Here we shall only emphasize two important propositions:

1. Every creation repeats the pre-eminent cosmogonic act, the Creation of the world.

2. Consequently, whatever is founded has its foundation at the center of the world (since, as we know, the Creation itself took place from a center).

[35] *Comentarii la legenda Meşterului Manole* (Bucharest, 1943).

Among the many examples at hand, we shall choose only one, which, as it is interesting in other respects too, will reappear later in our exposition. In India, before a single stone is laid, "The astrologer shows what spot in the foundation is exactly above the head of the snake that supports the world. The mason fashions a little wooden peg from the wood of the Khadira tree, and with a coconut drives the peg into the ground at this particular spot, in such a way as to peg the head of the snake securely down. . . . If this snake should ever shake its head really violently, it would shake the world to pieces." [36] A foundation stone is placed above the peg. The cornerstone is thus situated exactly at the "center of the world." But the act of foundation at the same time repeats the cosmogonic act, for to "secure" the snake's head, to drive the peg into it, is to imitate the primordial gesture of Soma (*Ṛg-Veda*, II, 12, 1) or of Indra when the latter "smote the Serpent in his lair" (VI, 17, 9), when his thunderbolt "cut off its head" (I, 52, 10). The serpent symbolizes chaos, the formless and nonmanifested. Indra comes upon Vṛtra (IV, 19, 3) undivided (*aparvan*), unawakened (*abudh-yam*), sleeping (*abudhyamānam*), sunk in deepest sleep (*suṣupaṇam*), outstretched (*aśayānam*). The hurling of the lightning and the decapitation are equivalent to the act of Creation, with passage from the nonmanifested to the manifested, from the formless to the formed. Vṛtra had confiscated the waters and was keeping them in the hollows of the mountains. This means either that Vṛtra was the absolute master—in the same manner as Tiamat or any serpent divinity—of all chaos before the Creation; or that the great serpent, keeping the waters for himself alone, had left the whole world ravaged by drought. Whether this confiscation occurred before the act of Creation or is to

---

[36] Mrs. (Margaret) Sinclair Stevenson, *The Rites of the Twice-Born* (London, 1920), p. 354 and note.

be placed after the foundation of the world, the meaning remains the same: Vṛtra "hinders" [37] the world from being made, or from enduring. Symbol of the nonmanifested, of the latent, or of the formless, Vṛtra represents the chaos which existed before the Creation.

In our commentaries on the legend of Master Manole (cf. note 35, above) we attempted to explain construction rites through imitation of the cosmogonic gesture. The theory that these rites imply comes down to this: nothing can endure if it is not "animated," if it is not, through a sacrifice, endowed with a "soul"; the prototype of the construction rite is the sacrifice that took place at the time of the foundation of the world. In fact, in certain archaic cosmogonies, the world was given existence through the sacrifice of a primordial monster, symbolizing chaos (Tiamat), or through that of a cosmic giant (Ymir, Pan-Ku, Puruṣa). To assure the reality and the enduringness of a construction, there is a repetition of the divine act of perfect construction: the Creation of the worlds and of man. As the first step, the "reality" of the site is secured through consecration of the ground, i.e., through its transformation into a center; then the validity of the act of construction is confirmed by repetition of the divine sacrifice. Naturally, the consecration of the center occurs in a space qualitatively different from profane space. Through the paradox of rite, every consecrated space coincides with the center of the world, just as the time of any ritual coincides with the mythical time of the "beginning." Through repetition of the cosmogonic act, concrete time, in which the construction takes place, is projected into mythical time, *in illo tempore* when the foundation of the world occurred. Thus the reality and the enduringness of a construction are

---

[37] Mephistopheles too was *der Vater aller Hindernisse*, "the father of all hindrances" (*Faust*, v. 6209).

assured not only by the transformation of profane space into a transcendent space (the center) but also by the transformation of concrete time into mythical time. Any ritual whatever, as we shall see later, unfolds not only in a consecrated space (i.e., one different in essence from profane space) but also in a "sacred time," "once upon a time" (*in illo tempore, ab origine*), that is, when the ritual was performed for the first time by a god, an ancestor, or a hero.

Divine Models of Rituals

EVERY RITUAL has a divine model, an archetype; this fact is well enough known for us to confine ourselves to recalling a few examples. "We must do what the gods did in the beginning" (*Śatapatha Brāhmaṇa*, VII, 2, 1, 4). "Thus the gods did; thus men do" (*Taittirīya Brāhmaṇa*, I, 5, 9, 4). This Indian adage summarizes all the theory underlying rituals in all countries. We find the theory among so-called primitive peoples no less than we do in developed cultures. The aborigines of southeastern Australia, for example, practice circumcision with a stone knife because it was thus that their ancestors taught them to do; the Amazulu Negroes do likewise because Unkulunkulu (civilizing hero) decreed *in illo tempore:* "Let men circumcise, that they may not be boys." [38] The hako ceremony of the Pawnee Indians was revealed to the priests by Tirawa, the supreme God, at the beginning of time. Among the Sakalavas of Madagascar, "all domestic, social, national, and religious customs and ceremonies must be observed in conformity with the *lilin-draza*, i.e., with the established customs and

[38] A. W. Howitt, *The Native Tribes of South-East Australia* (London, 1904), pp. 645 ff.; Henry Callaway, *The Religious System of the Amazulu* (London, 1869), p. 58.

21

unwritten laws inherited from the ancestors . . ." [39] It is useless to multiply examples; all religious acts are held to have been founded by gods, civilizing heroes, or mythical ancestors.[40] It may be mentioned in passing that, among primitives, not only do rituals have their mythical model but any human act whatever acquires effectiveness to the extent to which it exactly *repeats* an act performed at the beginning of time by a god, a hero, or an ancestor. We shall return at the end of this chapter to these model acts, which men only repeat again and again.

However, as we said, such a "theory" does not justify ritual only in primitive cultures. In the Egypt of the later centuries, for example, the power of rite and word possessed by the priests was due to imitation of the primordial gesture of the god Thoth, who had created the world by the force of his word. Iranian tradition knows that religious festivals were instituted by Ormazd to commemorate the stages of the cosmic Creation, which continued for a year. At the end of each period—representing, respectively, the creation of the sky, the waters, the earth, plants, animals, and man—Ormazd rested for five days, thus instituting the principal Mazdean festivals (cf. *Bundahišn*, I, A 18 ff.). Man only repeats the act of the Creation; his religious calendar commemorates, in the space of a year, all the cosmogonic phases which took place *ab origine*. In fact, the sacred year ceaselessly repeats the Creation; man is contemporary with the cosmogony and with the anthropogony because ritual projects him into the mythical epoch of the beginning. A bacchant, through his orgiastic rites, imitates the drama of the suffering Dionysos; an Orphic, through his initiation ceremonial, repeats the original gestures of Orpheus.

[39] Arnold van Gennep, *Tabou et totémisme à Madagascar* (Paris, 1904), pp. 27 ff.
[40] Cf. Gerardus van der Leeuw, *Phänomenologie der Religion* (Tübingen, 1933), pp. 349 ff., 360 ff.

The Judaeo-Christian Sabbath is also an *imitatio dei*.
The Sabbath rest reproduces the primordial gesture of the
Lord, for it was on the seventh day of the Creation that
God ". . . rested . . . from all his work which he had
made" (Genesis 2 : 2). The message of the Saviour is first
of all an example which demands imitation. After washing
his disciples' feet, Jesus said to them: "For I have given
you an example, that ye should do as I have done to you"
(John 13 : 15). Humility is only a virtue; but humility
practiced after the Saviour's example is a religious act and
a means of salvation: ". . . as I have loved you, that ye
also love one another" (John 13 : 34; 15 : 12). This Christian love is consecrated by the example of Jesus. Its actual
practice annuls the sin of the human condition and makes
man divine. He who believes in Jesus can do what He did;
his limitations and impotence are abolished. "He that be-
lieveth on me, the works that I do shall he do also . . ."
(John 14 : 12). The liturgy is precisely a commemoration
of the life and Passion of the Saviour. We shall see later
that this commemoration is in fact a reactualization of
those days.

Marriage rites too have a divine model, and human marriage reproduces the hierogamy, more especially the union
of heaven and earth. "I am Heaven," says the husband,
"thou art Earth" (*dyaur aham, pritivī tvam; Bṛhadāraṇyaka Upaniṣad*, VI, 4, 20). Even in Vedic times, husband
and bride are assimilated to heaven and earth (*Atharva-
Veda*, XIV, 2, 71), while in another hymn (*Atharva-Veda*,
XIV, 1) each nuptial gesture is justified by a prototype in
mythical times: "Wherewith Agni grasped the right hand
of this earth, therefore grasp I thy hand . . . Let god
Savitar grasp thy hand . . . Tvashtar disposed the gar-
ment for beauty, by direction of Bṛhaspati, of the poets;
therewith let Savitar and Bhaga envelop this woman, like

23

Sūrya, with progeny (48, 49, 52)."[41] In the procreation ritual transmitted by the *Bṛhadāraṇyaka Upaniṣad*, the generative act becomes a hierogamy of cosmic proportions, mobilizing a whole group of gods: "Let Viṣṇu make the womb prepared! Let Tvashṭri shape the various forms! Prajāpati—let him pour in! Let Dhātri place the germ for thee!" (VI, 4, 21).[42] Dido celebrates her marriage with Aeneas in the midst of a violent storm (Virgil, *Aeneid*, VI, 160); their union coincides with that of the elements; heaven embraces its bride, dispensing fertilizing rain. In Greece, marriage rites imitated the example of Zeus secretly uniting himself with Hera (Pausanias, II, 36, 2). Diodorus Siculus tells us that the Cretan hierogamy was imitated by the inhabitants of that island; in other words, the ceremonial union found its justification in a primordial event which occurred *in illo tempore*.

What must be emphasized is the cosmogonic structure of all these matrimonial rites: it is not merely a question of imitating an exemplary model, the hierogamy between heaven and earth; the principal consideration is the result of that hierogamy, i.e., the cosmic Creation. This is why, in Polynesia, when a sterile woman wants to be fecundated, she imitates the exemplary gesture of the Primordial Mother, who, *in illo tempore*, was laid on the ground by the great god, Io. And the cosmogonic myth is recited on the same occasion. In divorce proceedings, on the contrary, an incantation is chanted in which the "separation of heaven and earth" is invoked.[43] The ritual recitation of the cosmogonic myth on the occasion of marriages is current among numerous peoples; we shall return to it later. For

[41] W. D. Whitney and C. R. Lanman (trans.), *Atharva-Veda* (Harvard Oriental Series, VIII, Cambridge, Mass., 1905), pp. 750–51.

[42] R. E. Hume (trans.), *The Thirteen Principal Upanishads* (Oxford, 1931).

[43] Cf. E. S. C. Handy, *Polynesian Religion* (Honolulu, 1927), pp. 10 ff.; Raffaele Pettazzoni, "Io and Rangi," *Pro regno pro sanctuario* [in homage to G. van der Leeuw] (Nijkerk, 1950), pp. 359–60.

the moment let us point out that the cosmic myth serves as the exemplary model not only in the case of marriages but also in the case of any other ceremony whose end is the restoration of integral wholeness; this is why the myth of the Creation of the World is recited in connection with cures, fecundity, childbirth, agricultural activities, and so on. The cosmogony first of all represents Creation.

Demeter lay with Iasion on the newly sown ground, at the beginning of spring (*Odyssey*, V, 125). The meaning of this union is clear: it contributes to promoting the fertility of the soil, the prodigious surge of the forces of telluric creation. This practice was comparatively frequent, down to the last century, in northern and central Europe—witness the various customs of symbolic union between couples in the fields.[44] In China, young couples went out in spring and united on the grass in order to stimulate "cosmic regeneration" and "universal germination." In fact, every human union has its model and its justification in the hierogamy, the cosmic union of the elements. Book IV of the *Li Chi*, the "Yüeh Ling" (book of monthly regulations), specifies that his wives must present themselves to the emperor to cohabit with him in the first month of spring, when thunder is heard. Thus the cosmic example is followed by the sovereign and the whole people. Marital union is a rite integrated with the cosmic rhythm and validated by that integration.

The entire Paleo-Oriental symbolism of marriage can be explained through celestial models. The Sumerians celebrated the union of the elements on the day of the New Year; throughout the ancient East, the same day receives its luster not only from the myth of the hierogamy but also from the rites of the king's union with the goddess.[45] It is

[44] J. W. E. Mannhardt, *Wald- und Feldkulte*, I (2nd edn., Berlin, 1904–1905), pp. 169 ff., 180 ff.

[45] Cf. S. H. Hooke, ed., *Myth and Ritual* (London, 1935), pp. 9, 19, 34 ff.

on New Year's day that Ishtar lies with Tammuz, and the king reproduces this mythical hierogamy by consummating ritual union with the goddess (i.e., with the hierodule who represents her on earth) in a secret chamber of the temple, where the nuptial bed of the goddess stands. The divine union assures terrestrial fecundity; when Ninlil lies with Enlil, rain begins to fall.[46] The same fecundity is assured by the ceremonial union of the king, that of couples on earth, and so on. The world is regenerated each time the hierogamy is imitated, i.e., each time matrimonial union is accomplished. The German *Hochzeit* is derived from *Hochgezît*, New Year festival. Marriage regenerates the "year" and consequently confers fecundity, wealth, and happiness.

The assimilation of the sexual act to agricultural work is frequent in numerous cultures.[47] In the *Śatapatha Brāhmaṇa* (VII, 2, 2, 5) the earth is assimilated to the female organ of generation (*yoni*) and the seed to the *semen virile*. "Your women are your tilth, so come into your tillage how you choose" (Qur'ân, II, 223).[48] The majority of collective orgies find a ritual justification in fostering the forces of vegetation: they take place at certain critical periods of the year, e.g., when the seed sprouts or the harvests ripen, and always have a hierogamy as their mythical model. Such, for example, is the orgy practiced by the Ewe tribe (West Africa) at the time when the barley begins to sprout; the orgy is legitimized by a hierogamy (young girls are offered to the python god). We find this same legitimization among the Oraons; their orgy takes place in May, at the time of the union of the sun god with the earth goddess. All these orgiastic excesses find their

[46] René Labat, *Le Caractère religieux de la royauté assyro-babylonienne* (Paris, 1939), pp. 247 ff.; cf. the traces of a similar mythico-ritual complex in Israel: Patai, pp. 90 ff.

[47] See the chapter on agricultural mysticism in our *Patterns in Comparative Religion*, pp. 354 ff.

[48] Trans. E. H. Palmer, *Sacred Books of the East*, VI, p. 33.

justification, in one way or another, in a cosmic or bio-cosmic act: regeneration of the year, critical period of the harvest, and so forth. The boys who paraded naked through the streets of Rome at the Floralia (April 28) or who, at the Lupercalia, touched women to exorcise their sterility; the liberties permitted throughout India on the occasion of the Holi festival; the licentiousness which was the rule in central and northern Europe at the time of the harvest festival and against which the ecclesiastical authorities struggled so unavailingly [49]—all these manifestations also had a superhuman prototype and tended to institute universal fertility and abundance.[50]

For the purpose of this study, it is of no concern that we should know to what extent marriage rites and the orgy created the myths which justify them. What is important is that both the orgy and marriage constituted rituals imitating divine gestures or certain episodes of the sacred drama of the cosmos—the legitimization of human acts through an extrahuman model. If the myth sometimes followed the rite—for example, preconjugal ceremonial unions preceded the appearance of the myth of the preconjugal relations between Hera and Zeus, the myth which served to justify them—the fact in no wise lessens the sacred character of the ritual. The myth is "late" only as a formulation; but its content is archaic and refers to sacraments—that is, to acts which presuppose an absolute reality, a reality which is extrahuman.

Archetypes of Profane Activities

To SUMMARIZE, we might say that the archaic world knows nothing of "profane" activities: every act which has a

---

[49] Cf., for example, the Council of Auxerre in 590.
[50] On the cosmological significance of the orgy, see Ch. II.

definite meaning—hunting, fishing, agriculture; games, conflicts, sexuality,—in some way participates in the sacred. As we shall see more clearly later, the only profane activities are those which have no mythical meaning, that is, which lack exemplary models. Thus we may say that every responsible activity in pursuit of a definite end is, for the archaic world, a ritual. But since the majority of these activities have undergone a long process of desacralization and have, in modern societies, become profane, we have thought it proper to group them separately.

Take the dance, for example. All dances were originally sacred; in other words, they had an extrahuman model. The model may in some cases have been a totemic or emblematic animal, whose motions were reproduced to conjure up its concrete presence through magic, to increase its numbers, to obtain incorporation into the animal on the part of man. In other cases the model may have been revealed by a divinity (for example the pyrrhic, the martial dance created by Athena) or by a hero (cf. Theseus' dance in the Labyrinth). The dance may be executed to acquire food, to honor the dead, or to assure good order in the cosmos. It may take place upon the occasion of initiations, of magico-religious ceremonies, of marriages, and so on. But all these details need not be discussed here. What is of interest to us is its presumed extrahuman origin (for every dance was created *in illo tempore*, in the mythical period, by an ancestor, a totemic animal, a god, or a hero). Choreographic rhythms have their model outside of the profane life of man; whether they reproduce the movements of the totemic or emblematic animal, or the motions of the stars; whether they themselves constitute rituals (labyrinthine steps, leaps, gestures performed with ceremonial instruments)—a dance always imitates an archetypal gesture or commemorates a mythical moment. In a word, it is a repetition, and consequently a reactualization, of *illud tempus*, "those days."

Struggles, conflicts, and wars for the most part have a ritual cause and function. They are a stimulating opposition between the two halves of a clan, or a struggle between the representatives of two divinities (for example, in Egypt, the combat between two groups representing Osiris and Set); but this always commemorates an episode of the divine and cosmic drama. War or the duel can in no case be explained through rationalistic motives. Hocart has very rightly brought out the ritual role of hostilities.[51] Each time the conflict is repeated, there is imitation of an archetypal model. In Nordic tradition, the first duel took place when Thor, provoked by the giant Hrungnir, met him at the "frontier" and conquered him in single combat. The motif is found again in Indo-European mythology, and Georges Dumézil [52] rightly regards it as a late but authentic version of the very ancient scenario of a military initiation. The young warrior had to reproduce the combat between Thor and Hrungnir; in fact, the military initiation consists in an act of daring whose mythical prototype is the slaying of a three-headed monster. The frenzied *berserkir*, ferocious warriors, realized precisely the state of sacred fury (*wut, menos, furor*) of the primordial world.

The Indian ceremony of the consecration of a king, the *rājasūya*, "is only the terrestrial reproduction of the ancient consecration which Varuṇa, the first Sovereign, performed for his own benefit—as the *Brāhmaṇa* repeat again and again . . . All through the ritual exegeses, we find it tediously but instructively reiterated that if the king makes

[51] A. M. Hocart, *Le Progrès de l'homme* (French trans., Paris, 1935), pp. 188 ff., 319 ff.; cf. also W. C. MacLeod, *The Origin and History of Politics* (New York, 1931), pp. 217 ff.

[52] Cf. his *Mythes et dieux des Germains* (Paris, 1939), pp. 99 ff., and his *Horace et les Curiaces* (Paris, 1942), pp. 126 ff.

such and such a gesture, it is because in the dawn of time, on the day of his consecration, Varuṇa made it." [53] And this same mechanism can be shown to exist in all other traditions, so far as the available documentation permits.[54] Construction rituals repeat the primordial act of the cosmogonic construction. The sacrifice performed at the building of a house, church, bridge, is simply the imitation, on the human plane, of the sacrifice performed *in illo tempore* to give birth to the world.

As for the magical and pharmaceutical value of certain herbs, it too is due to a celestial prototype of the plant, or to the fact that it was first gathered by a god. No plant is precious in itself, but only through its participation in an archetype, or through the repetition of certain gestures and words which, by isolating it from profane space, consecrate it. Thus two formulas of incantation, used in England in the sixteenth century at the gathering of simples, state the origin of their therapeutic virtue: they grew for the first time (i.e., *ab origine*) on the sacred hill of Calvary, at the "center" of the Earth:

Haile be thou, holie hearbe, growing on the ground;/all in the mount Caluarie first wert thou found./Thou art good for manie a sore, and healest manie a wound;/in the name of sweet Jesus, I take thee from the ground [1584].

Hallowed be thou, Vervein [verbena], as thou growest on the ground,/for in the Mount of Calvary, there thou wast first found./Thou healedst our Saviour Jesus Christ, and staunchest his bleeding wound;/in the name of [Father, Son, Holy Ghost], I take thee from the ground [1608].

The effectiveness of these herbs is attributed to the fact that their prototypes were discovered at a decisive cosmic

[53] Dumézil, *Ouranôs-Váruṇa* (Paris, 1934), pp. 42, 62.
[54] Cf. Moret's classic studies of the sacred character of royalty in Egypt, and Labat's of Assyro-Babylonian royalty.

moment (*in illo tempore*) on Mount Calvary. They received their consecration for having healed the Redeemer's wounds. The virtue of gathered herbs is effective only insofar as the person gathering them repeats this primordial gesture of cure. This is why an old formula of incantation says: "We go to gather herbs to put them on the wounds of the Lord . . ." [55]

These formulas of popular Christian magic continue an ancient tradition. In India, for example, the herb *Kapitthaka* (*Feronia elephantum*) cures sexual impotence because, *ab origine*, the Gandharva used it to restore the virility of Varuṇa. Hence the ritual gathering of this herb is, in effect, a repetition of the Gandharva's act. "Thee that the Gandharva dug for Varuna whose virility was dead, thee here do we dig, a penis-erecting herb" (*Atharva-Veda* IV, 4, 1).[56] A long invocation in the *Papyrus magique de Paris* indicates the exceptional status of the herb gathered: "Thou wast sown by Cronos, received by Hera, preserved by Ammon, brought forth by Isis, nourished by rainy Zeus; thou grewest by grace of the Sun and dew . . ." For Christians, medicinal herbs owed their effectiveness to the fact that they were found for the first time on the mount of Calvary. For the ancients, herbs owed their curative virtues to the fact that they were first discovered by gods. "Betony, thou who wast first discovered by Aesculapius, or by the centaur Chiron . . ."—such is the invocation recommended by a treatise on herbs.[57]

It would be tedious, as well as purposeless, for this essay to mention the mythical prototypes of all human activities. The fact that human justice, for example, which is

[55] Ferdinand Ohrt, "Herba, gratiâ plena," *FF Communications* (Helsinki), No. 82 (1929), 17, 18; our "La Mandragore et le mythe de la 'naissance miraculeuse,'" *Zalmoxis* (Paris and Bucharest), III (1943), 1–52, particularly pp. 23 ff., and *Patterns in Comparative Religion*, pp. 296 ff.

[56] Trans. Whitney and Lanman, VII, p. 149.

[57] Armand Delatte, *Herbarius* (2nd edn., Liége, 1938), pp. 100, 102.

founded upon the idea of "law," has a celestial and transcendent model in the cosmic norms (*tao, artha, ṛta, tzedek, themis,* etc.) is too well known for us to insist upon it. That "works of human art are imitations of those of divine art" (*Aitareya Brāhmaṇa,* VI, 27) [58] is likewise a leitmotiv of archaic aesthetics, as Ananda K. Coomaraswamy's studies have admirably shown.[59] It is interesting to observe that the state of beatitude itself, *eudaimonia,* is an imitation of the divine condition, not to mention the various kinds of *enthousiasmos* created in the soul of man by the repetition of certain acts realized by the gods *in illo tempore* (Dionysiac orgy, etc.): "The Working of the Gods, eminent in blessedness, will be one apt for Contemplative Speculation: and of all human Workings that will have the greatest capacity for Happiness which is nearest akin to this" (Aristotle, *Nicomachean Ethics,* 1178b, 21); [60] "to become as like as possible to God" (Plato, *Theaetetus,* 176e); "haec hominis est perfectio, similitudo Dei" (St. Thomas Aquinas).

We must add that, for the traditional societies, all the important acts of life were revealed *ab origine* by gods or heroes. Men only repeat these exemplary and paradigmatic gestures *ad infinitum.* The Yuin tribe of Australia know that Daramulun, the "All Father," invented, for their especial benefit, all the utensils and arms that they have employed down to today. In the same way the Kurnai tribe know that Mungan-ngaua, the Supreme Being, lived among them, on earth, at the beginning of time, in order to teach them to make their implements, boats, weapons, "in fact, all the arts they know." [61] In New Guinea, many

[58] Cf. Plato, *Laws,* 667–69; *Statesman,* 306d, etc.
[59] See especially Coomaraswamy, "The Philosophy of Mediæval and Oriental Art," *Zalmoxis* (Paris and Bucharest), I (1938), 20–49, and *Figures of Speech or Figures of Thought* (London, 1946), pp. 29–96.
[60] Trans. D. P. Chase, *The Ethics of Aristotle,* (London, 1934).
[61] Howitt, pp. 543, 630.

myths tell of long sea voyages, "and thus they provide exemplars for the modern voyagers," as well as for all other activities, "whether of love, or war, or rain-making, or fishing, or whatever else . . . [Myth] gives precedents for the stages of construction, the tabu on sexual intercourse, etc." When a captain goes to sea, he personifies the mythical hero Aori. "He wears the costume which Aori is supposed to have worn, with a blackened face (and in a way prematurely) the same kind of *love* in his hair which Aori plucked from Iviri's head. He dances on the platform and extends his arms like Aori's wings . . . A man told me that when he went fish shooting (with bow and arrow) he pretended to be Kivavia himself." [62] He did not implore Kivavia's favor and help; he identified himself with the mythical hero.

This same symbolism of mythical precedents is to be found in other primitive cultures. In regard to the Karuk Indians of California, J. P. Harrington writes: "Everything that the Karuk did was enacted because the Ikxareyavs were believed to have set the example in story times The Ikxareyavs were the people who were in America before the Indians came. Modern Karuks, in a quandary now to render the word, volunteer such translations as 'the princes,' 'the chiefs,' 'the angels' . . . [These Ikxareyavs . . .] remaining with the Karuk only long enough to state and start all customs, telling them in every instance, 'Humans will do the same.' These doings and sayings are still related and quoted in the medicine formulas of the Karuk." [63]

The curious system of ritual commerce—the potlatch—which is found in the American Northwest, and to which

---

[62] F. E. Williams, cited by Lucien Lévy-Bruhl, *La Mythologie primitive* (Paris, 1935), pp. 162, 163–64.
[63] J. P. Harrington, cited by Lévy-Bruhl, p. 165.

Marcel Mauss has devoted a well-known study,[64] is only the repetition of a practice introduced by the ancestors in mythical times. It would be easy to multiply examples.[65]

Myths and History

EACH of the examples cited in the present chapter reveals the same "primitive" ontological conception: an object or an act becomes real only insofar as it imitates or repeats an archetype. Thus, reality is acquired solely through repetition or participation; everything which lacks an exemplary model is "meaningless," i.e., it lacks reality. Men would thus have a tendency to become archetypal and paradigmatic. This tendency may well appear paradoxical, in the sense that the man of a traditional culture sees himself as real only to the extent that he ceases to be himself (for a modern observer) and is satisfied with imitating and repeating the gestures of another. In other words, he sees himself as real, i.e., as "truly himself," only, and precisely, insofar as he ceases to be so. Hence it could be said that this "primitive" ontology has a Platonic structure; and in that case Plato could be regarded as the outstanding philosopher of "primitive mentality," that is, as the thinker who succeeded in giving philosophic currency and validity to the modes of life and behavior of archaic humanity. Obviously, this in no way lessens the originality of his philosophic genius; for his great title to our admiration remains his effort to justify this vision of archaic humanity the-

[64] Marcel Mauss, "Essai sur le don, forme archaïque de l'échange," *Année Sociologique* (Paris), I, 2nd series (1923–24).

[65] See, among others, Coomaraswamy's studies, "Vedic Exemplarism," *Harvard Journal of Asiatic Studies*, I (1936), 44–64, and *The Ṛg Veda as Land-náma-bók* (London, 1935).

oretically, through the dialectic means which the spirituality of his age made available to him.

But our interest here is not in this aspect of Platonic philosophy; it is in archaic ontology. Recognizing the Platonic structure of that ontology would not take us very far. No less important is the second conclusion to be drawn from analyzing the facts cited in the foregoing pages—that is, the abolition of time through the imitation of archetypes and the repetition of paradigmatic gestures. A sacrifice, for example, not only exactly reproduces the initial sacrifice revealed by a god *ab origine*, at the beginning of time, it also takes place at that same primordial mythical moment; in other words, every sacrifice repeats the initial sacrifice and coincides with it. All sacrifices are performed at the same mythical instant of the beginning; through the paradox of rite, profane time and duration are suspended. And the same holds true for all repetitions, i.e., all imitations of archetypes; through such imitation, man is projected into the mythical epoch in which the archetypes were first revealed. Thus we perceive a second aspect of primitive ontology: insofar as an act (or an object) acquires a certain reality through the repetition of certain paradigmatic gestures, and acquires it through that alone, there is an implicit abolition of profane time, of duration, of "history"; and he who reproduces the exemplary gesture thus finds himself transported into the mythical epoch in which its revelation took place.

The abolition of profane time and the individual's projection into mythical time do not occur, of course, except at essential periods—those, that is, when the individual is truly himself: on the occasion of rituals or of important acts (alimentation, generation, ceremonies, hunting, fishing, war, work). The rest of his life is passed in profane time, which is without meaning: in the state of "becoming."

Brahmanic texts clearly bring out the heterogeneity of these two times, the sacred and the profane, of the modality of the gods, which is coupled with immortality, and the modality of man, which is coupled with death. Insofar as he repeats the archetypal sacrifice, the sacrificer, in full ceremonial action, abandons the profane world of mortals and introduces himself into the divine world of the immortals. He himself, indeed, declares this, in the following terms: "I have attained Heaven, the gods; I am become immortal!" (*Taittirīya Saṃhitā*, I, 7, 9). Should he now descend once more to the profane world, which he has left during the rite, he would die instantly; hence various rites of desacralization are indispensable to restore the sacrificer to profane time. The same is true in the case of ceremonial sexual union; the individual ceases to live in profane and meaningless time, since he is imitating a divine archetype ("I am Heaven, thou art Earth," etc.). The Melanesian fisherman, when he goes to sea, becomes the hero Aori and is projected into mythical time, into the moment when the paradigmatic voyage took place. Just as profane space is abolished by the symbolism of the Center, which projects any temple, palace, or building into the same central point of mythical space, so any meaningful act performed by archaic man, any real act, i.e., any repetition of an archetypal gesture, suspends duration, abolishes profane time, and participates in mythical time.

This suspension of profane time answers to a profound need on the part of primitive man, as we shall have occasion to observe in the next chapter when we examine a series of parallel conceptions relating to the regeneration of time and the symbolism of the New Year. We shall then understand the significance of this need, and we shall see that the man of archaic cultures tolerates "history" with difficulty and attempts periodically to abolish it. The facts that we have examined in the present chapter will then acquire other meanings. But before entering upon the problem of the regeneration of time, we must look from another point of view at the mechanism of the transformation of man into archetype through repetition. We shall examine a definite case: to what extent does collective memory preserve the recollection of a historic event? We have seen that the warrior, whoever he may be, imitates a hero and seeks to approach this archetypal model as closely as possible. Let us now see what the memory of the people retains concerning a well-documented historical personage. By attacking the problem from this angle, we advance a step because in this instance we are dealing with a society which, though "popular," cannot be called primitive.

Thus, to give only one example, a familiar paradigmatic myth recounts the combat between the hero and a gigantic serpent, often three-headed, sometimes replaced by a marine monster (Indra, Herakles, and others; Marduk). Where tradition is still more or less a living thing, great monarchs consider themselves imitators of the primordial hero: Darius saw himself as a new Thraetona, the mythical Iranian hero who was said to have slain a three-headed monster; for him—and through him—history was regenerated, for it was in fact the revivification, the reactualization, of a primordial heroic myth. The Pharaoh's adversaries were considered "sons of ruin, wolves, dogs," and so forth. In the *Book of Apophis* the enemies whom the Pharaoh fights are identified with the dragon Apophis, while the Pharaoh himself is assimilated with the god Re, conqueror of the dragon.[66] The same transfiguration of history into myth, but from another point of view, is found in the visions of the Hebrew poets. In order to "tolerate

[66] Günther Roeder (ed.), *Urkunden zur Religion des alten Ägypten* (Jena, 1915), pp. 98 ff.

37

history," that is, to endure their military defeats and political humiliations, the Hebrews interpreted contemporary events by means of the very ancient cosmogonico-heroic myth, which, though it of course admitted the provisional victory of the dragon, above all implied the dragon's final extinction through a King-Messiah. Thus their imagination gives the Gentile kings (Zadokite Fragments, IX : 19–20) the characteristics of the dragon: such is the Pompey described in the Psalms of Solomon (IX : 29), the Nebuchadrezzar presented by Jeremiah (51 : 34). And in the Testament of Asher (VII : 3) the Messiah kills the dragon under water (cf. Psalm 74 : 13).

In the case of Darius and the Pharaoh, as in that of the Hebrew Messianic tradition, we are dealing with the conception of an "elite" who interpret contemporary history by means of a myth. A series of contemporary events is given an articulation and an interpretation that conform with the atemporal model of the heroic myth. For a hypercritical modern, Darius' pretention might signify boasting or political propaganda; the mythical transformation of the Gentile kings into dragons might represent a labored invention on the part of a Hebraic minority unable to tolerate "historical reality" and seeking to console themselves at any cost by taking refuge in myth and wishful thinking. That such an interpretation is erroneous, because it makes no allowance for the structure of archaic mentality, is shown, for one thing, by the fact that popular memory applies a strictly analogous process of articulation and interpretation to historical events and personages. If the transformation into myth of the biography of Alexander the Great may be suspected of having a literary origin, and consequently be accused of artificiality, the objection has no force in regard to the documents to which we shall now refer.

Dieudonné de Gozon, third Grand Master of the Knights of St. John at Rhodes, has remained famous for having slain the dragon of Malpasso. Legend, as was natural, bestowed on him the attributes of St. George, famed for his victorious fight with the monster. Needless to say, the documents of de Gozon's period make no reference to any such combat, and it does not begin to be mentioned until some two centuries after the hero's birth. In other words, by the simple fact that he was regarded as a hero, de Gozon was identified with a category, an archetype, which, entirely disregarding his real exploits, equipped him with a mythical biography from which it was *impossible* to omit combat with a reptilian monster.[67]

Petru Caraman, in a copiously documented study of the genesis of the historical ballad, shows that, of a definitely established historical event—the expedition against Poland by Malkoš Pasha in 1499, in an especially severe winter, which is mentioned in Leunclavius' chronicle as well as in other Polish sources, and during the course of which a whole Turkish army perished in Moldavia—the Romanian ballad that narrates the catastrophic Turkish expedition preserves almost nothing, the historical event having been completely translated into a mythical action (Malkoš Pasha fighting King Winter, etc.).[68]

This "mythicization" of historical personages appears in exactly the same way in Yugoslavian heroic poetry. Marko Kraljević, protagonist of the Yugoslavian epic, became famous for his courage during the second half of the fourteenth century. His historical existence is unquestionable, and we even know the date of his death (1394). But no sooner is Marko's historical personality received into

[67] Cf. the documentation in F. W. Hasluck, *Christianity and Islam under the Sultans*, II (Oxford, 1929), p. 649.

[68] Petru Caraman, "Geneza baladei istorice," *Anuarul Arhivei de Folklor* (Bucharest), I–II (1933–34).

the popular memory than it is abolished and his biography is reconstructed in accordance with the norms of myth. His mother is a *Vila*, a fairy, just as the Greek heroes were the sons of nymphs or naiads. His wife is also a *Vila*; he wins her through a ruse and takes great care to hide her wings lest she find them, take flight, and abandon him—as, by the way, in certain variants of the ballad, proves to be the case after the birth of their first child.[69] Marko fights a three-headed dragon and kills it, after the archetypal model of Indra, Thraetona, Herakles, and others.[70] In accordance with the myth of the enemy brothers, he too fights with his brother Andrija and kills him. Anachronisms abound in the cycle of Marko, as in all other archaic epic cycles. Marko, who died in 1394, is now the friend, now the enemy of John Hunyadi, who distinguished himself in the wars against the Turks *ca.* 1450.

It is interesting to note that these two heroes are brought together in the manuscripts of epic ballads of the seven-

[69] Cf. the myth of the Maori hero Tawhaki, whom his wife, a fairy come down to earth from heaven, abandons after giving him a child.

[70] This is not the place to enter upon the problem of the combat between monster and hero (cf. Bernhard Schweitzer, *Herakles*, Tübingen, 1922; A. Lods, *Comptes rendus de l'Académie des Inscriptions*, Paris, 1943, pp. 283 ff.). It is highly probable, as Georges Dumézil suggests (*Horace et les Curiaces*, Paris, 1942, especially pp. 126 ff.), that the hero's combat with a three-headed monster is the transformation into myth of an archaic initiation ritual. That this initiation does not always belong to the "heroic" type, appears, among other things, from the British Columbian parallels mentioned by Dumézil (pp. 129–30), where shamanic initiation is also involved. If, in Christian mythology, St. George fights and kills the dragon "heroically," other saints achieve the same result without fighting (cf. the French legends of St. Samson, St. Marguerite, St. Bié, etc.; Paul Sébillot, *Le Folk-lore de France*, I (Paris, 1904), p. 468; III (Paris, 1906), 298, 299. On the other hand, we must not forget that, apart from its possible role in the rites and myths of heroic initiation, the dragon, in many other traditions (East Asiatic, Indian, African, and others) is given a cosmological symbolism: it symbolizes the involution, the pre-formal modality, of the universe, the undivided "One" of pre-Creation (cf. Ananda K. Coomaraswamy, *The Darker Side of Dawn*, Washington, 1935; "Sir Gawain and the Green Knight: Indra and Namuci," *Speculum* (Cambridge, Mass.), Jan., 1944, pp. 1–23). This is why snakes and dragons are nearly everywhere identified with the "masters of the ground," with the autochthons against whom the newcomers, the "conquerors," those who are to form (i.e., create) the occupied territories, must fight. (On the assimilation of snakes and autochthons, cf. Charles Autran, *L'Epopée indoue*, Paris, 1946, pp. 66 ff.).

teenth century; that is, two centuries after Hunyadi's death. In modern epic poems, anachronisms are far less frequent.[71] The personages celebrated in them have not yet had time to be transformed into mythical heroes.

The same mythical prestige glorifies other heroes of Yugoslavian epic poetry. Vukašin and Novak marry *Vila*. Vuk (the "Dragon Despot") fights the dragon of Jastrebac and can himself turn into a dragon. Vuk, who reigned in Syrmia between 1471 and 1485, comes to the rescue of Lazar and Milica, who died about a century earlier. In the poems whose action centers upon the first battle of Kossovo (1389), persons figure who had been dead for twenty years (e.g., Vukašin) or who were not to die until a century later (Erceg Stjepan). Fairies (*Vila*) cure wounded heroes, resuscitate them, foretell the future to them, warn them of imminent dangers, just as in myth a female being aids and protects the hero. No heroic "ordeal" is omitted: shooting an arrow through an apple, jumping over several horses, recognizing a girl among a group of youths dressed alike, and so on.[72]

Certain heroes of the Russian *byliny* are most probably connected with historical prototypes. A number of the heroes of the Kiev cycle are mentioned in the chronicles. But with this their historicity ends. We cannot even determine whether the Prince Vladimir who forms the center of the Kiev cycle is Vladimir I, who died in 1015, or Vladimir II, who reigned from 1113 to 1125. As for the great heroes of the *byliny* of this cycle, Svyatogor, Mikula, and Volga, the historic elements preserved in their persons and adventures amount to almost nothing. They end by becoming indistinguishable from the heroes of myths and

---

[71] H. Munro and N. (Kershaw) Chadwick, *The Growth of Literature*, II (Cambridge, 1932–40), pp. 375 ff.

[72] See the texts and critical bibliography in Chadwick, II, pp. 309–42, 374–89, etc.

folk tales. One of the protagonists of the Kiev cycle, Dobrynya Nikitich, who sometimes appears in the *byliny* as Vladimir's nephew, owes his principal fame to a purely mythical exploit: he kills a twelve-headed dragon. Another hero of the *byliny*, St. Michael of Potuka, kills a dragon that is on the point of devouring a girl brought to it as an offering.

To a certain extent, we witness the metamorphosis of a historical figure into a mythical hero. We are not referring merely to the supernatural elements summoned to reinforce their legends: for example the hero Volga, of the Kiev cycle, changes into a bird or a wolf, exactly like a shaman or a figure of ancient legend; Egori is born with silver feet, golden arms, and his head covered with pearls; Ilya of Murom resembles a giant of folklore—he boasts that he can make heaven and earth touch. But there is something else: this mythicization of the historical prototypes who gave the popular epic songs their heroes takes place in accordance with an exemplary standard; they are "formed after the image" of the heroes of ancient myth. They all resemble one another in the fact of their miraculous birth; and, just as in the *Mahābhārata* and the Homeric poems, at least one of their parents is divine. As in the epic songs of the Tatars and the Polynesians, these heroes undertake a journey to heaven or descend into hell.

To repeat, the historical character of the persons celebrated in epic poetry is not in question. But their historicity does not long resist the corrosive action of mythicization. The historical event in itself, however important, does not remain in the popular memory, nor does its recollection kindle the poetic imagination save insofar as the particular historical event closely approaches a mythical model. In the *bylina* devoted to the catastrophes of the Napoleonic invasion of 1812, the role of Czar Alexander I as head of the army has been forgotten, as have the name and the importance of Borodino; all that survives is the figure of Kutusov in the guise of a popular hero. In 1912, an entire Serbian brigade saw Marko Kraljević lead the charge against the castle of Prilep, which, centuries earlier, had been that popular hero's fief: a particularly heroic exploit provided sufficient occasion for the popular imagination to seize upon it and assimilate it to the traditional archetype of Marko's exploits, the more so because his own castle was at stake.

"Myth is the last—not the first—stage in the development of a hero." [73] But this only confirms the conclusion reached by many investigators (Caraman and others): the recollection of a historical event or a real personage survives in popular memory for two or three centuries at the utmost. This is because popular memory finds difficulty in retaining individual events and real figures. The structures by means of which it functions are different: categories instead of events, archetypes instead of historical personages. The historical personage is assimilated to his mythical model (hero, etc.), while the event is identified with the category of mythical actions (fight with a monster, enemy brothers, etc.). If certain epic poems preserve what is called "historical truth," this truth almost never has to do with definite persons and events, but with institutions, customs, landscapes. Thus, for example, as Murko observes, the Serbian epic poems quite accurately describe life on the Austrian-Turkish and Turkish-Venetian frontier before the Peace of Karlowitz in 1699.[74] But such "historical truths" are not concerned with personalities or events, but

[73] Chadwick, III, p. 762.

[74] Matthias Murko, *La Poésie populaire épique en Yougoslavie au début du XX* siècle* (Paris, 1929), p. 29. An examination of the historical and mythical elements in the Germanic, Celtic, Scandinavian, and other epic literatures does not fall within the scope of this study. On this subject, the reader may refer to the Chadwicks' three volumes.

with traditional forms of social and political life (the "becoming" of which is slower than the "becoming" of the individual)—in a word, with archetypes.

The memory of the collectivity is anhistorical. This statement implies neither a popular origin for folklore nor a collective creation for epic poetry. Murko, Chadwick, and other investigators have brought out the role of the creative personality, of the "artist," in the invention and development of epic poetry. We wish to say no more than that—quite apart from the origin of folklore themes and from the greater or lesser degree of talent in the creators of epic poetry—the memory of historical events is modified, after two or three centuries, in such a way that it can enter into the mold of the archaic mentality, which cannot accept what is individual and preserves only what is exemplary. This reduction of events to categories and of individuals to archetypes, carried out by the consciousness of the popular strata in Europe almost down to our day, is performed in conformity with archaic ontology. We might say that popular memory restores to the historical personage of modern times its meaning as imitator of the archetype and reproducer of archetypal gestures—a meaning of which the members of archaic societies have always been, and continue to be, conscious (as the examples cited in this chapter show), but which has been forgotten by such personages as Dieudonné de Gozon or Marko Kraljević.

Sometimes, though very rarely, an investigator chances to come upon the actual transformation of an event into myth. Just before the last war, the Romanian folklorist Constantin Brailoiu had occasion to record an admirable ballad in a village in Maramureş. Its subject was a tragedy of love: the young suitor had been bewitched by a mountain fairy, and a few days before he was to be married, the fairy, driven by jealousy, had flung him from a cliff. The next day, shepherds found his body and, caught in a tree, his hat. They carried the body back to the village and his fiancée came to meet them; upon seeing her lover dead, she poured out a funeral lament, full of mythological allusions, a liturgical text of rustic beauty. Such was the content of the ballad. In the course of recording the variants that he was able to collect, the folklorist tried to learn the period when the tragedy had occurred; he was told that it was a very old story, which had happened "long ago." Pursuing his inquiries, however, he learned that the event had taken place not quite forty years earlier. He finally even discovered that the heroine was still alive. He went to see her and heard the story from her own lips. It was a quite commonplace tragedy: one evening her lover had slipped and fallen over a cliff; he had not died instantly; his cries had been heard by mountaineers; he had been carried to the village, where he had died soon after. At the funeral, his fiancée, with the other women of the village, had repeated the customary ritual lamentations, without the slightest allusion to the mountain fairy.

Thus, despite the presence of the principal witness, a few years had sufficed to strip the event of all historical authenticity, to transform it into a legendary tale: the jealous fairy, the murder of the young man, the discovery of the dead body, the lament, rich in mythological themes, chanted by the fiancée. Almost all the people of the village had been contemporaries of the authentic historical fact; but this fact, as such, could not satisfy them: the tragic death of a young man on the eve of his marriage was something different from a simple death by accident; it had an occult meaning that could only be revealed by its identification with the category of myth. The mythicization of the accident had not stopped at the creation of a ballad; people told the story of the jealous fairy even when they were talking freely, "prosaically," of the young man's death. When the folklorist drew the villagers' attention to the authentic version, they replied that the old woman had forgotten; that her great grief had almost destroyed her mind. It was the myth that told the truth: the real story was already only a falsification. Besides, was not the myth truer by the fact that it made the real story yield a deeper and richer meaning, revealing a tragic destiny?

THE ANHISTORICAL CHARACTER of popular memory, the inability of collective memory to retain historical events and individuals except insofar as it transforms them into archetypes—that is, insofar as it annuls all their historical and personal peculiarities—pose a series of new problems, which we are obliged to set aside for the moment. But at this point we have the right to ask ourselves if the importance of archetypes for the consciousness of archaic man, and the inability of popular memory to retain anything but archetypes, do not reveal to us something more than the resistance to history exhibited by traditional spirituality; if this mnemonic lacuna does not reveal the transitoriness, or at least the secondary character, of human individuality as such—that individuality whose creative spontaneity, in the last analysis, constitutes the authenticity and irreversibility of history. In any case, it is remarkable that, on the one hand, popular memory refuses to preserve the personal, historical elements of a hero's biography while, on the other hand, higher mystical experiences imply a final elevation of the personal God to the transpersonal God. It would also be instructive to compare, from this point of view, the conceptions of life after death that have been elaborated by various traditions. The transformation of the dead person into an "ancestor"

46

corresponds to the fusion of the individual into an archetypal category. In numerous traditions (in Greece, for example) the souls of the common dead no longer possess a "memory"; that is, they lose what may be called their historical individuality. The transformation of the dead into ghosts, and so on, in a certain sense signifies their reidentification with the impersonal archetype of the ancestor. The fact that in the Greek tradition only heroes preserve their personality (i.e., their memory) after death, is easy to understand: having, in his life on earth, performed no actions which were not exemplary, the hero retains the memory of them, since, from a certain point of view, these acts were impersonal.

Leaving aside the conceptions of the transformation of the dead into "ancestors," and regarding the fact of death as a concluding of the "history" of the individual, it still seems very natural that the post-mortem memory of that history should be limited or, in other words, that the memory of passions, of events, of all that is connected with the individual strictly speaking, comes to an end at a certain moment of his existence after death. As for the objection that an impersonal survival is equivalent to a real death (inasmuch as only the personality and the memory that are connected with duration and history can be called a survival), it is valid only from the point of view of a "historical consciousness," in other words, from the point of view of modern man, for archaic consciousness accords no importance to personal memories. It is not easy to define what such a "survival of impersonal consciousness" might mean, although certain spiritual experiences afford a glimpse. What is personal and historical in the emotion we feel when we listen to the music of Bach, in the attention necessary for the solution of a mathematical problem, in the concentrated lucidity presupposed by the examination of any philosophical question? Insofar as he allows himself to be influenced by history, modern man feels himself diminished by the possibility of this impersonal survival. But interest in the "irreversible" and the "new" in history is a recent discovery in the life of humanity. On the contrary, archaic humanity, as we shall presently see, defended itself, to the utmost of its powers, against all the novelty and irreversibility which history entails.

CHAPTER TWO

THE REGENERATION OF TIME

Year, New Year, Cosmogony · Periodicity of the
Creation · Continuous Regeneration of Time

*

Year, New Year, Cosmogony

THE rites and beliefs here grouped under "Regeneration of Time" afford an endless variety, and we are under little illusion as to the possibility of fitting them into a coherent and unified system. In any case, the present essay requires neither an exposition of all the forms this regeneration assumes nor a morphological and historical analysis of them. Our aim is not to learn how the calendar came to be constituted, nor to discover how far it might be possible to work out a system that would comprehend the conceptions of the "year" held by various peoples. In most primitive societies, the New Year is equivalent to the raising of the taboo on the new harvest, which is thus declared edible and innoxious for the whole community. Where several species of grains or fruits are cultivated, ripening successively at different seasons, we sometimes find several New Year festivals.[1] This means the divisions of time are determined by the rituals that govern the renewal of alimentary reserves; that is, the rituals that guarantee the continuity of the life of the community in its entirety. (This does not justify any conclusion that these rituals are simple reflexes of economic and social life: in traditional societies, the "economic" and the "social" bear an entirely different meaning from that which a modern European tends to give them.) The adoption of the solar year as the unit of time is of Egyptian origin. The majority of other historical cultures—and Egypt itself down to a certain period—had a year, at once lunar and solar, of 360 days (that is, 12 months of 30 days each), to which five intercalary days were added.[2] The Zuñi Indians called

---

[1] Martin P. Nilsson, *Primitive Time Reckoning* (Acta Societatis Humaniorum Litterarum Lundensis, I, Lund, 1920), p. 270.

[2] Cf. F. Rock, "Das Jahr von 360 Tagen und seine Gliederung," *Wiener Beiträge zur Kulturgeschichte und Linguistik*, I (1930), 253–88.

the months the "steps of the year" and the year the "passage of time." The beginning of the year varied from country to country as well as in different periods, calendar reforms being constantly introduced to make the ritual meaning of festivals fit the seasons with which it was supposed to correspond.

However, neither the instability and latitude in the beginning of the New Year (March–April, July 19—as in ancient Egypt—September, October, December–January, etc.) nor the different lengths attributed to the year by different peoples were able to lessen the importance attached, in all countries, to the end of a period of time and the beginning of a new period. Hence, as will easily be understood, it is a matter of indifference to us that, for example, the African Yoruba divide the year into dry season and rainy season and that among them the week numbers five days as against eight days for the Bakoto; or that the Barundi distribute the months by lunations and thus arrive at a year of about thirteen months; or, again, that the Ashanti divide each month into two periods of ten days (or of nine days and a half). For us, the essential thing is that there is everywhere a conception of the end and the beginning of a temporal period, based on the observation of biocosmic rhythms and forming part of a larger system— the system of periodic purifications (cf. purges, fasting, confession of sins, etc.) and of the periodic regeneration of life. This need for a periodic regeneration seems to us of considerable significance in itself. Yet the examples that we shall presently adduce will show us something even more important, namely, that a periodic regeneration of time presupposes, in more or less explicit form—and especially in the historical civilizations—a new Creation, that is, a repetition of the cosmogonic act. And this conception of a periodic creation, i.e., of the cyclical regeneration of time, poses the problem of the abolition of "history," the problem which is our prime concern in this essay.

Readers familiar with ethnography and the history of religions are well aware of the importance of a whole series of periodic ceremonies, which, for convenience, we can group under two main headings: (1) annual expulsion of demons, diseases, and sins; (2) rituals of the days preceding and following the New Year. In the part of *The Golden Bough* entitled *The Scapegoat*, Sir James George Frazer has, in his fashion, brought together a sufficient number of facts in the two categories. There can be no question of repeating this documentation in the following pages. In broad outline, the ceremony of expelling demons, diseases, and sins can be reduced to the following elements: fasting, ablutions, and purifications; extinguishing the fire and ritually rekindling it in a second part of the ceremonial; expulsion of demons by means of noises, cries, blows (indoors), followed by their pursuit through the village with uproar and hullabaloo; this expulsion can be practiced under the form of the ritual sending away of an animal (type "scapegoat") or of a man (type Mamurius Veturius), regarded as the material vehicle through which the faults of the entire community are transported beyond the limits of the territory it inhabits (the scapegoat was driven "into the desert" by the Hebrews and the Babylonians). There are often ceremonial combats between two groups of actors, or collective orgies, or processions of masked men (representing the souls of the ancestors, the gods, and so forth). In many places the belief still survives that, at the time of these manifestations, the souls of the dead approach the houses of the living, who respectfully go out to meet them and lavish honors upon them for several days, after which they are led to the boundary of the village in procession or are driven from it. It is at the same period that the ceremonies of the initiation of young men are performed (we have definite proofs of this among the Japanese, the Hopi Indians, certain Indo-European peoples, and others; see below, pp. 66 ff.). Almost everywhere the expulsion of demons, diseases, and sins coincides—or at one period coincided—with the festival of the New Year.

Naturally, we seldom find all these elements together in explicit conjunction; in certain societies the ceremonies of extinguishing and rekindling the fire predominate; in others, it is the material expulsion (by noise and violent gestures) of demons and diseases; in yet others, the expulsion of the scapegoat in human or animal form. But the meaning of the whole ceremony, like that of each of its constituent elements, is sufficiently clear: on the occasion of the division of time into independent units, "years," we witness not only the effectual cessation of a certain temporal interval and the beginning of another, but also the abolition of the past year and of past time. And this is the meaning of ritual purifications: a combustion, an annulling of the sins and faults of the individual and of those of the community as a whole—not a mere "purifying." Regeneration, as its name indicates, is a new birth. The examples cited in the preceding chapter, and especially those which we are now to review, clearly show that this annual expulsion of sins, diseases, and demons is basically an attempt to restore—if only momentarily—mythical and primordial time, "pure" time, the time of the "instant" of the Creation. Every New Year is a resumption of time from the beginning, that is, a repetition of the cosmogony. The ritual combats between two groups of actors, the presence of the dead, the Saturnalia, and the orgies are so many elements which—for reasons we shall soon set forth—denote that at the end of the year and in the expectation of the New Year there is a repetition of the mythical moment of the passage from chaos to cosmos.

The ceremonial for the Babylonian New Year, the *akîtu*, is sufficiently conclusive in this respect. *Akîtu* could be celebrated at the spring equinox, in the month of Nisan, as well as at the autumnal equinox, in the month of Tišrît (derived from *šurru*, "to begin"). The antiquity of this ceremonial admits of no doubt, even if the dates at which it was celebrated were variable. Its ideology and its ritual structure existed as early as the Sumerian period, and the system of the *akîtu* has been identified from Akkadian times.[3] These chronological details are not without importance; we are dealing with documents of the earliest "historical" civilization, in which the sovereign played a considerable role, since he was regarded as the son and vicar of the divinity on earth; as such, he was responsible for the regularity of the rhythms of nature and for the good estate of the entire society. Hence it is not surprising to find him playing an important role in the ceremonial of the New Year; upon him fell the duty of regenerating time.

During the course of the *akîtu* ceremony, which lasted twelve days, the so-called epic of the Creation, *Enûma eliš*, was solemnly recited several times in the temple of Marduk. Thus the combat between Marduk and the sea monster Tiamat was reactualized—the combat that had taken place *in illo tempore* and had put an end to chaos by the final victory of the god.[4] Marduk creates the cosmos from the fragments of Tiamat's torn body and creates man from the blood of the demon Kingu, to whom Tiamat had entrusted the Tablets of Destiny (*Enûma eliš*, VI, 33).[5] That this commemoration of the Creation was in effect a

[3] C. F. Jean, *La Religion sumérienne* (Paris, 1931), p. 168; Henri Frankfort, "Gods and Myths in Sargonid Seals," *Iraq* (London), I (1934), pp. 21 ff.

[4] The same among the Hittites, where the exemplary combat between the hurricane god Tešup and the serpent Illuyankaš was recited and reactualized within the frame of the New Year festival. Cf. Albrecht Götze, *Kleinasien* (Leipzig, 1933), p. 130; Giuseppe Furlani, *La Religione degli Hittiti* (Bologna, 1936), p. 89.

[5] The motif of creation by means of the body of a primordial being occurs in other cultures: in China, India, and Iran, and among the Germanic tribes.

reactualization of the cosmogonic act is proved both by the rituals and by the formulas recited during the course of the ceremony. The combat between Tiamat and Marduk was mimed by a struggle between two groups of actors, a ceremonial that is also found among the Hittites (again in the frame of the dramatic scenario of the New Year), among the Egyptians, and at Ras Shamra.[6] The struggle between two groups of actors not only commemorated the primordial conflict between Marduk and Tiamat; it repeated, it actualized, the cosmogony, the passage from chaos to cosmos. The mythical event was present: "May he continue to conquer Tiamat and shorten her days!" the celebrant exclaimed. The combat, the victory, and the Creation took place *at that very moment.*

It is also within the frame of the same *akîtu* ceremonial that the festival called the "festival of the fates," Zagmuk, was celebrated, in which the omens for each of the twelve months of the year were determined, which was equivalent to creating the twelve months to come (a ritual that has been preserved, more or less explicitly, in other traditions; see below, pp. 65 ff.). To Marduk's descent into hell (the god was a "prisoner in the mountain," i.e., in the infernal regions) there corresponded a period of mourning and fasting for the whole community and of "humiliation" for the king, a ritual that formed part of a great carnival system into which we cannot enter here. It was at the same period that the expulsion of evils and sins took place by means of a scapegoat. The cycle was closed by the god's

---

[6] René Labat, *Le Caractère religieux de la royauté assyro-babylonienne* (Paris, 1939), p. 99; Götze, pp. 130 ff.; Ivan Engnell, *Studies in Divine Kingship in the Ancient Near East* (Uppsala, 1943), pp. 11, 101. There are also traces of a ritual combat at Jerusalem; see below, p. 60. A similar combat took place in the Hippodrome of Constantinople down to the last centuries of the Byzantine Empire; Joannes Malalas speaks of it in his *Chronographia* (Bonn, 1831, pp. 173–76) and Benjamin of Tudela also mentions it; see Raphael Patai, *Man and Temple* (London, 1947), pp. 77 ff.

hierogamy with Sarpanītū, a hierogamy that was reproduced by the king and a hierodule in the chamber of the
goddess and to which there certainly corresponded a period
of collective orgy.[7]

As we see, the *akîtu* festival comprises a series of dramatic elements the intention of which is the abolition of
past time, the restoration of primordial chaos, and the
repetition of the cosmogonic act:

1. The first act of the ceremony represents the domi-
nation of Tiamat and thus marks a regression into the
mythical period before the Creation; all forms are supposed
to be confounded in the marine abyss of the beginning, the
apsu. Enthronement of a "carnival" king, "humiliation"
of the real sovereign, overturning of the entire social order
(according to Berossus, the slaves became the masters,
and so on)—every feature suggests universal confusion,
the abolition of order and hierarchy, "orgy," chaos. We
witness, one might say, a "deluge" that annihilates all
humanity in order to prepare the way for a new and
regenerated human species. In addition, does not the Babylonian tradition of the Deluge, as preserved in Tablet XI
of the Epic of Gilgamesh, tell us that Ut-napistim, before
embarking in the ship which he had built in order to escape
the Deluge, had organized a festival "as on the day of the

[7] Documentary material, interpretation, and bibliography in Heinrich Zimmern,
"Zum babylonische Neujahrsfest," I–II, *Berichte über die Verhandlungen der Königlich Sächsichen Gesellschaft der Wissenschaften* (Leipzig), *Phil.-hist. Klasse,* LVIII
(1906); LXX (1918); S. A. Pallis, *The Babylonian Akîtu Festival* (Copenhagen,
1926); see also H. S. Nyberg's criticisms in the *Monde Oriental* (Uppsala), XXIII
(1929), 204–11; Raffaele Pettazzoni, "Der babylonische Ritus des Akitu und das
Gedicht der Weltschöpfung," *Eranos-Jahrbuch,* XIX (Zurich, 1950), pp. 403–30.
On Zagmuk and the Babylonian Saturnalia, cf. Sir James George Frazer, *The Scapegoat* (Part VI of *The Golden Bough,* London, 1907–15), pp. 356 ff.; Labat, pp. 95 ff.;
a rash attempt to see in the Babylonian ceremonial the source of all other similar
rituals found in the Mediterranean basin, Asia, northern and central Europe, in
Waldemar Liungman, *Traditionswanderungen, Euphrat-Rhein,* I–II (Helsinki,
1937–38), pp. 290 ff. and passim. Cf. also S. H. Hooke, *The Origins of Early Semitic
Ritual* (London, 1938), pp. 57 ff. For the same New Year ritual in Tibet, see
Robert Bleichsteiner, *L'Église jaune* (French trans., Paris, 1937), pp. 231 ff.

New Year (*akîtu*)"? We shall find this deluge element—sometimes a mere water element—in certain other traditions.

2. The creation of the world, which took place, *in illo tempore*, at the beginning of the year, is thus reactualized each year.

3. Man participates directly, though to a reduced extent, in this cosmogonic work (struggle between the two groups of actors representing Marduk and Tiamat; "mysteries" celebrated on certain occasions, according to the interpretation of Zimmern and Reitzenstein [8]); this participation, as we saw in the preceding chapter, projects him into mythical time, making him contemporary with the cosmogony.

4. The "festival of the fates" is also a formula of creation, in which the "fate" of each month and each day is decided.

5. The hierogamy is a concrete realization of the "rebirth" of the world and man.

The meaning and the ritual of the Babylonian New Year have their counterparts throughout the Paleo-Oriental world. We have noted a few of these in passing, but the list is far from being exhausted. In a remarkable study, which has not aroused the interest it deserves, the Dutch scholar A. J. Wensinck has demonstrated the symmetry between various mythico-ceremonial systems of the New Year throughout the Semitic world; in each of these systems we find the same central idea of the yearly return to chaos, followed by a new creation. [9] Wensinck has rightly discerned the cosmic character of the New Year rituals (with all due reservations in regard to his theory of the

[8] But cf. also Efraim Briem, *Les Sociétés secrètes des mystères* (trans. from the Swedish by E. Guerre, Paris, 1941), p. 131.

[9] A. J. Wensinck, "The Semitic New Year and the Origin of Eschatology," *Acta Orientalia* (Lund), I (1923), pp. 158–99.

"origin" of this ritualo-cosmic conception, which he tries to find in the periodic spectacle of the disappearance and reappearance of vegetation; the fact is that, for "primitives," nature is a hierophany, and the "laws of nature" are the revelation of the mode of existence of the divinity). That the deluge and, in general, the element of water are present, in one way or another, in the ritual of the New Year is sufficiently proved by the libations practiced on this occasion and by the relations between this ritual and the rains. "In Tišrît was the world created," says Rabbi Eliezer; "in Nisan," affirms Rabbi Josua. Now, both these are rainy months.[10] It is at the time of the Feast of Tabernacles that the quantity of rain allotted for the coming year is settled, i.e., that the "fate" of the months to come is determined.[11] Christ blesses the waters on Epiphany, while Easter and New Year's Day were the habitual dates for baptism in primitive Christianity. (Baptism is equivalent to the ritual death of the old man followed by a new birth. On the cosmic level, it is equivalent to the deluge: abolition of contours, fusion of all forms, return to the formless.) Ephraem Syrus rightly discerned the mystery of this yearly repetition of the Creation and attempted to explain it: "He has created the heavens anew, because sinners have worshipped all the heavenly bodies; has created the world anew, which had been withered by Adam, a new creation arose from His spittle." [12]

Certain traces of the ancient scenario of the combat and the victory of the divinity over the marine monster, incarnation of chaos, can also be discerned in the Jewish ceremonial of the New Year, as it has been preserved in

[10] Ibid., p. 168. See further texts in Patai, pp. 68 ff.
[11] *Rosh Hashshana*, I, 2; Wensinck, p. 163; Patai, pp. 24 ff. Rabbi Ishmael and Rabbi Akiba agree on this point: that the Feast of Tabernacles is the time when the quantity of the rains for the coming year is decided in heaven; cf. Patai, p. 41.
[12] *Hymns on Epiphany*, VIII, 16; Wensinck, p. 169.

the Jerusalem cultus. Recent studies (Mowinckel, Pedersen, Hans Schmidt, A. R. Johnson, for example) have defined the ritual elements and the cosmogonico-eschatological implications of the Psalms and have shown the role played by the king in the New Year festival, which commemorated the triumph of Yahweh, leader of the forces of l' ght, over the forces of darkness (the chaos of the sea, the primordial monster Rahab). This triumph was followed by the enthronement of Yahweh as king and the repetition of the cosmogonic act. The slaying of the monster Rahab and the victory over the waters (signifying the organization of the world) were equivalent to the creation of the cosmos and at the same time to the "salvation" of man (victory over "death," guarantee of food for the coming year, and so on).[13] Of these various traces of archaic cults, let us for the moment bear in mind only the periodic repetition (at the "revolution of the year," Exodus 34 : 22; at the "going out" of the year, 23 : 16) of the Creation; for the combat with Rahab presupposes the reactualization of primordial chaos, while the victory over the waters can only signify the establishment of "stable forms," i.e., the Creation. We shall see later that in the consciousness of the Hebrew people this cosmogonic victory becomes victory over foreign kings present and to come; the cosmogony justifies Messianism and the Apocalypse, and thus lays the foundations for a philosophy of history.

The fact that this periodic "salvation" of man finds an immediate counterpart in the guarantee of food for the year to come (consecration of the new harvest) must not be allowed to hypnotize us to the point of seeing in this ceremonial only the traces of a primitive agrarian festival.

---

[13] Cf. A. R. Johnson, "The Rôle of the King in the Jerusalem Cultus," in *The Labyrinth*, ed. S. H. Hooke (London, 1935), pp. 79 ff.; see also Patai, pp. 73 ff.

Indeed, on the one hand, alimentation had a ritual meaning in all archaic societies; what we call "vital values" was rather the expression of an ontology in biological terms; for archaic man, life is an absolute reality, and, as such, it is sacred. On the other hand, the New Year, the Feast of Tabernacles so called (*hag hasuk-kôt*), pre-eminently the festival of Yahweh (Judges 21 : 19; Leviticus 23 : 39; etc.), took place on the fifteenth day of the seventh month (Deuteronomy 16 : 13; Zechariah 14 : 16), that is, five days after the *iôm ha-kippûrîm* (Leviticus 16 : 29) and its ceremonial of the scapegoat. Now it is difficult to separate these two religious moments, the elimination of the sins of the collectivity and the festival of the New Year, especially if we bear in mind that, before the adoption of the Babylonian calendar, the seventh month was the *first* month in the Jewish calendar. It was customary, at the time of the *iôm ha-kippûrîm*, for the girls to go outside the boundaries of the village or town to dance and amuse themselves, and it was on this occasion that marriages were arranged. But it was also on this day that freedom was allowed to a number of excesses, sometimes even orgiastic, which remind us both of the final phase of the *akîtu* (also celebrated outside the town) and of the various forms of license that were the rule almost everywhere in the frame of New Year ceremonials.[14]

Marriages, sexual license, collective purification through confession of sins and expulsion of the scapegoat, consecration of the new harvest, enthronement of Yahweh and commemoration of his victory over "death," were so many moments of an extensive ceremonial system. The ambivalence and polarity of these episodes (fasting and excess, grief and joy, despair and orgy) only confirm their

[14] See the references of the Talmud to orgiastic excesses in Raffaele Pettazzoni, *La confessione dei peccati*, II (Bologna, 1935), p. 229. Same state of affairs at Hierapolis; cf. Lucian, *De dea Syra*, 20; Patai, pp. 71 ff.

complementary function in the frame of the same system. But the chief moments indubitably remain the purification through the scapegoat and the repetition of the cosmogonic act by Yahweh; all the rest is only the application, on different planes answering to different needs, of the same archetypal gesture: the regeneration of the world and life through repetition of the cosmogony.

Periodicity of the Creation

THE CREATION of the world, then, is reproduced every year. Allah is he who effects the creation, hence he repeats it (*Qur'ân*, X, 4 f.). This eternal repetition of the cosmogonic act, by transforming every New Year into the inauguration of an era, permits the return of the dead to life, and maintains the hope of the faithful in the resurrection of the body. We shall soon return to the relations between the New Year ceremonies and the cult of the dead. At this point let us note that the beliefs, held almost everywhere, according to which the dead return to their families (and often return as "living dead") at the New Year season (during the twelve days between Christmas and Epiphany) signify the hope that the abolition of time is possible at this mythical moment, in which the world is destroyed and re-created. The dead can come back now, for all barriers between the dead and the living are broken (is not primordial chaos reactualized?), and they will come back because at this paradoxical instant time will be suspended, hence they can again be contemporaries of the living. Moreover, since a new Creation is then in preparation, they can hope for a return to life that will be enduring and concrete.

This is why, where belief in the resurrection of the body

62

is prevalent, it is also believed that it will take place at the beginning of the year, that is, at the opening of a new epoch. Lehmann and Pedersen have shown this for the Semitic peoples, while Wensinck [15] has collected copious evidence for it in the Christian tradition. For example: "The Almighty awakens the bodies (at Epiphany) together with the spirits." [16] A Pahlavi text given by Darmesteter says: "It is in the month Fravardīn, on the day Xurdāth, that the Lord Ormazd will produce the resurrection and the 'second body' and that the world will be saved from impotence with the demons, the drŭgs, etc. And there will be abundance everywhere; there will be no more want of food; the world will be pure, man liberated from the opposition [of the evil spirit] and immortal for ever." [17] Qazwīnī, for his part, says that, on the day of Nawrôz, God resuscitated the dead "and he gave them back their souls, and he gave his orders to the sky, which shed rain upon them, and thus it is that people have adopted the custom of pouring water on that day." [18] The very close connections between the ideas of Creation through water (aquatic cosmogony, deluge that periodically regenerates historical life, rain), birth, and resurrection are confirmed by this saying from the Talmud: "God hath three keys, of rain, of birth, of rising of the dead." [19]

The symbolic repetition of the Creation in the setting of the New Year festival has been preserved down to our times among the Mandaeans of Iraq and Iran. Even today, at the beginning of the year the Tatars of Persia plant seed in a jar filled with earth; they do it, they say, in memory of the Creation. The custom of sowing seed at the time

[15] Op. cit., p. 171.

[16] Ephraem Syrus, I, 1.

[17] James Darmesteter, Le Zend-Avesta, II (Paris, 1892), p. 640, note 138.

[18] Cosmography, cited by Arthur Christensen, Les Types du premier homme et du premier roi dans l'histoire légendaire des Iraniens, II (Stockholm, 1917), p. 147.

[19] Ta'anit, fol. 2a; Wensinck, p. 173.

of the spring equinox (we must remember that March marked the beginning of the year in numerous civilizations) is found over a very extensive area and has always been linked with agricultural ceremonies.[20] But the drama of vegetation enters into the symbolism of the periodic regeneration of nature and man. Agriculture is only one of the planes upon which the symbolism of periodic regeneration applies. And if the popular and empiric character of the "agricultural version" of this symbolism has enabled it to attain an extreme dissemination, that version can in no case be regarded as the principle and intent of the complex symbolism of periodic regeneration. That symbolism has its foundation in lunar mysticism; hence, from the ethnographic point of view, we are able to recognize it even in preagrarian societies. What is primordial and essential is the idea of regeneration, that is, of repetition of the Creation.

The custom of the Tatars of Persia must, then, be fitted into the Iranian cosmo-eschatological system that presupposes it and explains it. The Nawrôz, the Persian New Year, is at once the festival of Ahuramazda (celebrated on the day "Ormazd" of the first month) and the day on which the Creation of the world and of man took place.[21] It is on the day of Nawrôz that "renovating the creation" takes place.[22] According to the tradition transmitted by Dimasqī,[23] the king proclaimed: "Here is a new day of a new month of a new year; what time has wasted must be

[20] E. S. Drower (E. S. Stevens), *The Mandaeans of Iraq and Iran* (Oxford, 1937), p. 86; H. Lassy, *Muharram Mysteries* (Helsinki, 1916), pp. 219, 223. Cf. Sir James George Frazer, *Adonis, Attis, Osiris: Studies in the History of Oriental Religion* (3d edn., London, 1914), pp. 252 ff.; and, more recently, Liungman, I, pp. 103 ff., who attempts to derive this custom from Osirian rituals.

[21] See the texts collected by Josef Marquart, "The Nawrôz, Its History and Its Significance," *Journal of the Cama Oriental Institute* (Bombay), XXXI (1937), 1–51, especially pp. 16 ff. The original German text of this article was published in the *Dr. Modi Memorial Volume: Papers on Indo-Iranian and Other Subjects* (Bombay, 1930), pp. 709–65.

[22] Muhammad ibn Ahmad al-Bīrūnī, *The Chronology of Ancient Nations* (trans. C. Edward Sachau, London, 1879), p. 199.

[23] Christensen, II, p. 148.

renewed." It is on this day too that the fate of men is fixed for a whole year.[24] On the night of Nawrôz, innumerable fires and lights are to be seen,[25] and purifications by water and libations are performed to ensure abundant rains for the coming year.[26] Moreover, at the time of the "great Nawrôz" it was the custom for everyone to sow seven kinds of seed in a jar "and from their growth they drew conclusions regarding the corn of that year." [27] This custom is similar to the "fixing of fates" of the Babylonian New Year, a "fixing of fates" that has been perpetuated down to our day in the New Year ceremonials of the Mandaeans and the Yezedis.[28] It is also because the New Year repeats the cosmogonic act that the twelve days between Christmas and Epiphany are still regarded today as a prefiguration of the twelve months of the year. The peasants of Europe have no other reason for their universal practice of determining the weather of each month and its quota of rain in accordance with the meteorological signs of these twelve days.[29] We hardly need remind ourselves that it was at the Feast of Tabernacles that the quantity of rain assigned to each month was determined. For their part, the Indians of the Vedic era set apart the twelve days of midwinter as an image and replica of the year (*Ṛg-Veda*, IV, 33, 7).

However, in certain places and at certain periods, especially in the calendar of Darius, the Iranians recognized yet

[24] al-Bīrūnī, p. 201; Qazwīnī, trans. Christensen, II, p. 148.

[25] al-Bīrūnī, p. 200.

[26] Ibid., pp. 202–203.

[27] Ibid., p. 202. On the Nawrôz ceremonies in the nineteenth century, see Jakob Eduard Polak, *Persien. Das Land und seine Bewohner*, I (Leipzig, 1865), pp. 367 ff. Similar ideas are found among the Jews; as early as the Talmudic period the following words were spoken in the New Year prayer: "This day is the beginning of year works, a remembrance of the first day" (*Rosh Hashshana*, 27a; cited by Patai, p. 69).

[28] Cf. Drower, p. 87; Giuseppe Furlani, *Religione dei Yezidi* (Bologna, 1930), pp. 59 ff.

[29] Cf. Frazer, *The Scapegoat*, pp. 215 ff.; Georges Dumézil, *Le Problème des centaures* (Paris, 1929), pp. 39 ff.; Émile Nourry (P. Saintyves, pseud.), *L'Astrologie populaire* (Paris, 1937), pp. 61 ff. See also Marcel Granet, *La Pensée chinoise* (Paris, 1934), p. 107.

another New Year's Day, Mihragān, the festival of Mithra, which fell in the middle of summer. The Persian theologians, says al-Bīrūnī, "consider Mihragān as a sign of resurrection and the end of the world, because at Mihragān that which grows reaches its perfection and has no more material for further growth, and because animals cease from sexual intercourse. In the same way they make Nawrôz a sign for the beginning of the world, because the contrary of all these things happens on Nawrôz." [30] The end of the past year and the beginning of a new year are interpreted, in the tradition transmitted by al-Bīrūnī, as an exhaustion of biological resources on all cosmic planes, a veritable end of the world. (The "end of the world," i.e., of a particular historical cycle, is not always occasioned by a deluge, but also arises through fire, heat, etc. A magnificent apocalyptic vision, in which summer, with its scorching heat, is conceived as a return to chaos, is found in Isaiah 34 : 4, 9–11. Cf. similar images in *Bahman-Yašt*, II, 41; and Lactantius, *Divinae Institutiones*, VII, 16, 6.) [31]

In his *Le Problème des centaures*, Professor Georges Dumézil has studied the scenario of the end and the beginning of the year in a considerable part of the Indo-European world (Slavs, Iranians, Indians, Greco-Romans) and has distinguished the elements deriving from initiation ceremonies and preserved, in more or less corrupt form, by mythology and folklore. From an examination of the myths and rites of the Germanic secret societies and *Männerbunde*, Otto Höfler has drawn similar conclusions as to the importance of the twelve intercalary days and especially of New Year's Day. For his part, Waldemar Liungman has

[30] al-Bīrūnī, p. 208.

[31] Texts commented upon by Franz Cumont, "La Fin du monde selon les mages occidentaux," *Revue de l'Histoire des Religions* (Paris), Jan.–June, 1931, pp. 76 ff. Cf. also Wilhelm Bousset, *Der Antichrist in der Überlieferung des Judentums, des Neuen Testaments und der alten Kirche* (Göttingen, 1895), pp. 129 ff.

made the fire rites of the beginning of the year and the scenario of the carnival proceedings during these twelve days the subject of an extensive investigation, with the orientation and results of which we are, however, not always in agreement. We may also mention the researches of Otto Huth and J. Hertel, who, applying themselves to Roman and Vedic data, have especially insisted upon their motifs of renewal of the world through rekindling of the fire at the winter solstice, a renewal that is equivalent to a new creation.[32] For the purposes of the present essay, we shall recall only a few characteristic facts: (1) the twelve intermediate days prefigure the twelve months of the year (see also the rites mentioned above); (2) during the twelve corresponding nights, the dead come in procession to visit their families (apparition of the horse, pre-eminently the funerary animal, on the last night of the year; presence of the chthonico-funerary divinities Holda, Perchta, "Wilde Heer," etc., during these twelve nights), and this visit often (among the Germanic peoples and the Japanese) occurs in the frame of the ceremonial of the male secret societies; [33] (3) it is at this period that fires are extinguished and rekindled; [34] and finally (4) this is the moment of initiations, one of whose essential elements is precisely this extinction and rekindling of fire.[35] In this same

[32] Otto Höfler, *Kultische Geheimbünde der Germanen*, I (Frankfort on the Main, 1934); Liungman, II, pp. 426 ff. and passim; Otto Huth, *Janus* (Bonn, 1932); Johannes Hertel, *Das indogermanische Neujahrsopfer in Veda* (Leipzig, 1938).

[33] Höfler, op. cit.; Alexander Slawik, "Kultische Geheimbünde der Japaner und Germanen," *Wiener Beiträge zur Kulturgeschichte und Linguistik* (Salzburg and Leipzig), IV (1936), 675–764. In the ancient Near East there was a similar belief that the dead returned to earth on the occasion of seasonal festivities; cf. T. H. Gaster, *Thespis; Ritual, Myth and Drama in the Ancient Near East* (New York, 1950), pp. 28 ff.

[34] Émile Nourry (P. Saintyves, pseud.), *Essais de folklore biblique* (Paris, 1923), pp. 30 ff.; Hertel, p. 52; Dumézil, *Le Problème des Centaures*, p. 146; Huth, p. 146; Marcel Granet, *Danses et légendes de la Chine ancienne*, I–II (Paris, 1926), p. 155; Luigi Vannicelli, *La religione dei Lolo* (Milan, 1944), p. 80; Liungman, pp. 473 ff.

[35] Cf. Dumézil, pp. 148 ff. and passim. Among the Hopi, initiations always take place at the New Year; cf. Lewis Spence in Hastings' *Encyclopaedia of Religion and Ethics*, III, p. 67.

mythico-ceremonial complex of the end of the past year and the beginning of the New Year, we must also include the following facts: (5) ritual combats between two opposing groups (see above, pp. 53 ff.); and (6) presence of the erotic element (pursuit of girls, "Gandharvic" marriages, orgies; above, pp. 61 f.).

Each of these mythico-ritual motifs testifies to the wholly exceptional character of the days that precede and follow the first day of the year, although the eschato-cosmological function of the New Year (abolition of past time and repetition of the Creation) is not explicitly stated, except in the rites of prefiguration of the months and in the extinction and rekindling of fire. Nevertheless, this function can be shown to be implicit in all the rest of these mythico-ritual motifs. How could the invasion by the souls of the dead, for example, be anything but the sign of a suspension of profane time, the paradoxical realization of a coexistence of "past" and "present"? This coexistence is never so complete as at a period of chaos when all modalities coincide. The last days of the past year can be identified with the pre-Creation chaos, both through this invasion of the dead—which annuls the law of time—and through the sexual excesses which commonly mark the occasion. Even if, as the result of successive calendar reforms, the Saturnalia finally no longer coincided with the end and the beginning of the year, they nevertheless continued to mark the abolition of all norms and, in their violence, to illustrate an overturning of values (e.g., exchange of condition between masters and slaves, women treated as courtesans) and a general license, an orgiastic modality of society, in a word a reversion of all forms to indeterminate unity. The very locus appropriated to orgies among primitive peoples, preferably at the critical moments of the harvest (when the seed was buried in the ground), confirms this symmetry between the dissolution of the "form" (here the seed) in the soil and that of "social forms" in the orgiastic chaos.[36] On the vegetable as on the human plane, we are in the presence of a return to the primordial unity, to the inauguration of a "nocturnal" regime in which limits, contours, distances, are indiscernible.

The ritual extinguishing of fires is to be attributed to the same tendency to put an end to existing forms (worn away by the fact of their own existence) in order to make room for the birth of a new form, issuing from a new Creation. The ritual combats between two groups of actors reactualize the cosmogonic moment of the fight between the god and the primordial dragon (the serpent almost everywhere symbolizing what is latent, preformal, undifferentiated). Finally, the coincidence of initiations— in which the lighting of the "new fire" plays an especially important part—with the period of the New Year is explained both by the presence of the dead (secret and initiatory societies being at the same time representatives of the ancestors) and by the very structure of these ceremonies, which always suppose a "death" and a "resurrection," a "new birth," a "new man." It would be impossible to find a more appropriate frame for the initiation rituals than the twelve nights when the past year vanishes to give place to another year, another era: that is, to the period when, through the reactualization of the Creation, the world in effect begins.

Documented among almost all the Indo-European peoples, these mythico-ritual scenarios of the New Year—

---

[36] Of course, the role of the orgy in agricultural societies is far more complex. Sexual excesses exercised a magical influence on the coming harvest. But it is always possible to trace in it the tendency toward a violent fusion of all forms, in other words toward the reactualization of the pre-Creation chaos. See the chapter on fertility cults in our *Patterns in Comparative Religion* (English trans., London and New York, 1958), pp. 331 ff.

with their entire train of carnival masks, their funerary animals, their secret societies—were doubtless organized in their essential lines as early as the period of the Indo-European community. But such scenarios, or at least the aspects that we have emphasized in the present essay, cannot be regarded as an exclusively Indo-European creation. Centuries before the appearance of the Indo-Europeans in Asia Minor, the mythico-ritual complex of the New Year, regarded as repetition of the Creation, was known to the Sumero-Akkadians, and important elements of it are found among the Egyptians and the Hebrews. Since the genesis of mythico-ritual forms does not concern us here, we can content ourselves with the convenient hypothesis according to which these two ethnic groups (peoples of the Near East and Indo-Europeans) already possessed them in their prehistoric traditions. This hypothesis, by the way, is made even more plausible by the fact that an analogous system has been discovered in an eccentric culture: that of Japan. Dr. Slawik has studied the symmetries between the Japanese and the German secret organizations and has brought out an impressive number of parallel facts.[37] In Japan, as among the Germans (and among other Indo-European peoples), the last night of the year is marked by the appearance of funerary animals (horses, etc.), and of the chthonico-funerary gods and goddesses; it is then that the masked processions of the secret societies take place, that the dead visit the living, and that initiations are performed. Such secret societies are very old in Japan [38] and any influence from the Semitic East or of Indo-European origin appears to be excluded, at least in our present state of knowledge. All that can be

[37] Slawik, op. cit.
[38] Ibid., p. 762.

said, Slawik prudently notes, is that in the West as in the East of Eurasia, the cult complex of the "visitor" (souls of the dead, gods, and so on) developed before the historical period. This is one more confirmation of the archaic character of the New Year ceremonials.

At the same time, Japanese tradition has preserved the memory of a conception that is connected with the ceremonials of the year's end and that we may perhaps classify under the head of mystical psycho-physiology. Using the findings of the Japanese ethnographer Dr. Masao Oka,[39] Slawik situates the ceremonials of the secret societies in what he calls the *tama* complex. This *tama* is a spiritual substance that is found in man, in the souls of the dead, and in "holy men," and that, when winter passes into spring, becomes agitated and attempts to leave the body, while it impels the dead toward the dwellings of the living (cult complex of the visitor). It is to prevent this forsaking of the body by the *tama* that, according to Slawik's interpretation,[40] the festivals designed to hold or fix this spiritual substance are celebrated. It is probable that one of the purposes of the ceremonials of the end and the beginning of the year is likewise the "fixation" of the *tama*. Of this Japanese mystical psycho-physiology we shall, however, stress in particular the sense of annual crisis: the *tama's* tendency to become agitated and quit its normal condition when winter passes into spring (that is, during the last days of the ending year and the first days of the beginning year) is simply an elementary physiological formulation of retrogression into the nondistinct, of the reactualization of chaos. In this annual crisis of the *tama*, the primitive's experience finds a presage of the inevitable

[39] "Kulturschichten in Altjapan," German translation (still unpublished) from Dr. Masao Oka's Japanese MS.

[40] Slawik, pp. 679 ff.

71

confusion that is to put an end to a particular historical epoch in order to permit its renewal and regeneration, that is, in order to resume history at its beginning.

We shall further cite the group of periodical ceremonies practiced by the Karuk, Yurok, and Hupa tribes of California, ceremonies known by the names "New Year," "world's restoration," or "repair." The institution of the rites is attributed to mythical and immortal beings who inhabited the earth before mankind; it is these immortal beings who had first performed the ceremonies of the "world's renewal" and in exactly the places where mortals perform them today. "The esoteric magic and avowed purpose of the focal ceremonies comprising the system," Kroeber writes, "include reestablishment or firming of the earth, first-fruits observances, new fire, prevention of disease and calamity for another year or biennium." Hence we here have to do with an annual repetition of the cosmogonic ceremony inaugurated, *in illo tempore*, by immortal beings; for among the symbolic gestures performed, one of the most important is what the tribesmen call "putting posts under the world," and the ceremony coincides with the last moonless night and the appearance of the new moon, which implies the re-creation of the world. The fact that the New Year rite also includes the raising of the interdict upon the new harvest also confirms that we are dealing with a wholly new beginning of life.[41]

[41] P. E. Goddard, *Life and Culture of the Hupa* (University of California Publications in American Archaeology and Ethnology, Berkeley, 1903, I, No. 1), pp. 82 ff.; A. L. Kroeber, *Handbook of the Indians of California* (Washington, 1925), pp. 53 ff.; A. L. Kroeber and E. W. Gifford, *World Renewal, a Cult System of Native Northwest California* (Anthropological Records, XIII, No. 1, University of California, 1949), pp. 1 ff., 105 ff. Elsewhere in America the Deluge is annually commemorated; i.e., there is a *reactualization* of the great catastrophe that put an end to mankind except for the mythical ancestor; cf. Sir James George Frazer, *Folklore in the Old Testament*, I (London, 1918), pp. 293 ff. On the myth of the destruction and periodic re-creation of the world in archaic cultures, see F. R. Lehmann, "Weltuntergang und Welterneuerung im Glauben schriftloser Völker," *Zeitschrift für Ethnologie* (Berlin), LXXI (1939).

In connection with this "world's restoration," it is instructive to recall the ideology at the base of what has been called the ghost-dance religion; this mystical movement, which seized upon the North American tribes toward the end of the nineteenth century, prophesied the approach of universal regeneration, that is, the imminence of the end of the world, followed by the restoration of a paradisiacal earth. The ghost-dance religion is too complex to be summarized in a few lines, but for our purposes it will suffice to say that it attempted to hasten the end of the world by a massive and collective communication with the dead, achieved after dances that continued for four or five days without intermission. The dead invaded the earth, communicated with the living, and thus created a "confusion" that announced the close of the current cosmic cycle. But since the mythical visions of the "beginning" and the "end" of time are homologues—eschatology, at least in certain aspects, becoming one with cosmogony—the *eschaton* of the ghost-dance religion reactualized the mythical *illud tempus* of Paradise, of primordial plenitude.[42]

Continuous Regeneration of Time

THE HETEROGENEOUS nature of the material reviewed in the preceding pages need cause the reader no uneasiness. We have no intention of drawing any sort of ethnographic conclusion from this rapid exposition. Our sole aim has been a summary phenomenological analysis of these periodic purification rites (expulsion of demons, diseases, and sins) and of the ceremonials of the end and beginning of the year. That within each group of analogous beliefs there

[42] Cf. our *Shamanism: Archaic Techniques of Ecstasy* (English trans., New York and London, 1964), pp. 320 ff.

are variations, differences, incompatibilities, that the origin and dissemination of these ceremonials raise a host of problems requiring further study, we are the first to admit. It is for this very reason that we have avoided any kind of sociological or ethnographic interpretation and have limited ourselves to a simple exposition of the general meaning that emanates from all these ceremonials. In short, our ambition is to understand their meaning, to endeavor to see what they show us—leaving to possible future studies the detailed examination (genetic or historical) of each separate mythico-ritual complex.

It goes without saying that there are—we should almost feel justified in writing that there *must* be—very considerable differences between the various groups of periodic ceremonies, if only for the simple reason that we are dealing with both historical and "anhistorical" peoples or strata, with what are generally called "civilized man" and "primitive man." It is further of interest to note that the New Year scenarios in which the Creation is repeated are particularly explicit among the historical peoples, those with whom history, properly speaking, begins—that is, the Babylonians, Egyptians, Hebrews, Iranians. It almost seems that these peoples, conscious that they were the first to build "history," recorded their own acts for the use of their successors (not, however, without inevitable transfigurations in the matter of categories and archetypes, as we have seen in the preceding chapter). These same peoples also appear to have felt a deeper need to regenerate themselves periodically by abolishing past time and reactualizing the cosmogony.

As for the primitive societies that still live in the paradise of archetypes and for whom time is recorded only biologically without being allowed to become "history"— that is, without its corrosive action being able to exert itself upon consciousness by revealing the irreversibility of events—these primitive societies regenerate themselves periodically through expulsion of "evils" and confession of sins. The need these societies also feel for a periodic regeneration is a proof that they too cannot perpetually maintain their position in what we have just called the paradise of archetypes, and that their memory is capable (though doubtless far less intensely than that of a modern man) of revealing the irreversibility of events, that is, of recording history. Thus, among these primitive peoples too, the existence of man in the cosmos is regarded as a fall. The vast and monotonous morphology of the confession of sins, authoritatively studied by R. Pettazzoni in *La confessione dei peccati*, shows us that, even in the simplest human societies, "historical" memory, that is, the recollection of events that derive from no archetype, the recollection of personal events ("sins" in the majority of cases), is intolerable. We know that the beginning of the avowal of sins was a magical conception of eliminating a fault through some physical means (blood, speech, and so forth). But again it is not the confessional procedure in itself that interests us—it is magical in structure—but primitive man's need to free himself from the recollection of sin, i.e., of a succession of personal events that, taken together, constitute history.

Thus we observe the immense importance that collective regeneration through repetition of the cosmogonic act acquired among the peoples who created history. We might point out here that, for reasons which, of course, are various, but also because of the metaphysical and anhistorical structure of Indian spirituality, the Indians never elaborated a cosmological New Year scenario as extensive as those found in the ancient Near East. We might also point out that an outstandingly historical people, the Romans,

75

were continuously obsessed by the "end of Rome" and
sought innumerable systems of *renovatio*. But for the moment we do not wish to set the reader on this path. Hence
we shall limit ourselves to pointing out that, aside from
these periodic ceremonies of abolishing history, the traditional societies (that is, all societies down to those which
make up the modern world) knew and applied still other
methods intended to bring about the regeneration of time.

We have shown elsewhere [43] that construction rituals
likewise presuppose the more or less explicit imitation of
the cosmogonic act. For traditional man, the imitation of
an archetypal model is a reactualization of the mythical
moment when the archetype was revealed for the first
time. Consequently, these ceremonies too, which are
neither periodic nor collective, suspend the flow of profane
time, of duration, and project the celebrant into a mythical
time, *in illo tempore*. We have seen that all rituals imitate
a divine archetype and that their continual reactualization
takes place in one and the same atemporal mythical instant.
However, the construction rites show us something beyond
this: imitation, hence reactualization, of the cosmogony. A
"new era" opens with the building of every house. Every
construction is an absolute beginning; that is, tends to
restore the initial instant, the plenitude of a present that
contains no trace of history. Of course, the construction
rituals found in our day are in great part survivals, and
it is difficult to determine to what extent they are accompanied by an experience in the consciousness of the persons who observe them. But this rationalistic objection
is negligible. What is important is that man has felt the
need to reproduce the cosmogony in his constructions,
whatever be their nature; that this reproduction made him

---

[43] *Comentarii la legenda Meșterului Manole* (Bucharest, 1943); see also the preceding chapter.

contemporary with the mythical moment of the beginning of the world and that he felt the need of returning to that moment, as often as possible, in order to regenerate himself. It would require a most uncommon degree of perspicacity for anyone to be able to say to what extent those who, in the modern world, continue to repeat construction rituals still share in their meaning and their mystery. Doubtless their experiences are, on the whole, profane: the New Year signalized by a construction is translated into a new stage in the life of those who are to live in the house. But the structure of the myth and the rite remains unaltered by any of this, even if the experiences aroused by their actualization are no longer anything but profane: a construction is a new organization of the world and life. All that is needed is a modern man with a sensibility less closed to the miracle of life; and the experience of renewal would revive for him when he built a house or entered it for the first time (just as, even in the modern world, the New Year still preserves the prestige of the end of a past and the fresh beginning of a new life).

In many cases the available documents are sufficiently explicit: the construction of a sanctuary or a sacrificial altar repeats the cosmogony, and not only because the sanctuary represents the world but also because it incarnates the various temporal cycles. Here, for example, is what Flavius Josephus [44] has to tell us on the subject in connection with the traditional symbolism of the Temple of Jerusalem: the three parts of the sanctuary correspond to the three cosmic regions (the court representing the sea—that is, the lower regions—the Holy Place the earth, and the Holy of Holies heaven); the twelve loaves on the table are the twelve months of the year; the candelabrum with seventy branches represents the decans. The builders

[44] *Antiquities of the Jews*, III, 7, 7.

of the Temple not only constructed the world; they also constructed cosmic time.

The construction of cosmic time through repetition of the cosmogony is still more clearly brought out by the symbolism of Brahmanic sacrifice. Each Brahmanic sacrifice marks a new Creation of the world (cf., for example, *Śatapatha Brāhmaṇa*, VI, 5, 1 ff.). Indeed, the construction of the sacrificial altar is conceived as a "Creation of the world." The water with which the clay is mixed is the primordial water; the clay that forms the base of the altar is the earth; the side walls represent the atmosphere. Furthermore, each stage in the building of the altar is accompanied by verses in which the cosmic region that has just been created is explicitly named (*Śatapatha Brāhmaṇa*, I, 9, 2, 29; VI, 5, 1 ff.; 7, 2, 12; 7, 3, 1; 7, 3, 9). But if the raising of the altar imitates the cosmogonic act, the sacrifice proper has another end: to restore the primordial unity, that which existed before the Creation. For Prajāpati created the cosmos from his own substance; and once he had given it forth, "he feared death" (X, 4, 2, 2) and the gods brought him offerings to restore and revive him. In just the same way, he who today celebrates the sacrifice reproduces this primordial restoration of Prajāpati. "Thus whosoever, knowing this, performs this holy work, or he who but knows this [without practicing any ritual] makes up this Prajāpati whole and complete" (X, 4, 3, 24, etc.).[45] The sacrificer's conscious effort to re-establish the primordial unity, that is, to restore the *whole* that preceded the Creation, is a very important characteristic of the Indian spirit with its thirst for primordial unity, but we cannot pause to consider it. Let it suffice that we have found that, with every sacrifice, the Brahman

---

[45] Trans. Julius Eggeling, in *The Sacred Books of the East*, XLIII (Oxford, 1897), p. 361.

reactualizes the archetypal cosmogonic act, and that this coincidence between the "mythical instant" and the "present moment" supposes both the abolition of profane time and the continual regeneration of the world.

In effect, if "Prajāpati is the Year" (*Aitareya Brāhmaṇa*, VII, 7, 2, etc.), "the Year is the same as Death; and whosoever knows this Year (to be) Death, his life that (year) does not destroy . . ." (*Śatapatha Brāhmaṇa*, X, 4, 3, 1).[46] The Vedic altar, to employ Paul Mus' apt formula, is time materialized. "That fire-altar also is the Year,— the nights are its enclosing stones, and there are three hundred and sixty of these, because there are three hundred and sixty nights in the year; and the days are its yagushmati bricks, for there are three hundred and sixty of these, and three hundred and sixty days in the year" (X, 5, 4, 10).[47] At a certain moment in the construction of the altar, two bricks called "of the seasons" (*ṛtavyā*) are laid, and the text comments: "And as to why he lays down these two in this (layer):—this Agni (fire-altar) is the year . . . Again, . . . this fire-altar is Prajāpati, and Prajāpati is the year" (VIII, 2, 1, 17–18).[48] To reconstruct Prajāpati by means of a Vedic altar is also to reconstruct cosmic time. "Of five layers consists the fire-altar (each layer is a season), five seasons are a year, and the year is Agni (the altar) . . . And that Prajāpati who became relaxed is the year; and those five bodily parts of his which became relaxed are the seasons; for there are five seasons, and five are those layers: when he builds up the five layers, he thereby builds him up with the seasons . . . And those five bodily parts of his, the seasons, which became relaxed, are the regions (or quarters; i.e., the four cardinal points of the compass and the upper region); for

[46] Trans. ibid., p. 356.
[47] Trans., p. 386.
[48] Trans., p 29–30.

five in number are the regions, and five those layers: when he builds up the five layers, he builds him up with the regions" (VI, 8, 1, 15; 1, 2, 18 ff.).[49] Thus, with the construction of each new Vedic altar, not only is the cosmogony repeated and Prajāpati revived, but the year is constructed; that is, time is regenerated by being "created" anew.

The English anthropologist A. M. Hocart, in his brilliant and controversial book *Kingship*, has studied the ceremonial of the enthronement of the king among a number of civilized and primitive peoples and compared them with initiation rituals (which he regards as derived from the scenario of the royal ritual). That initiation is a "new birth," which includes a ritual death and resurrection, has long been known. But we are indebted to Hocart for identifying the initiatory elements of the coronation ceremonial and thus establishing suggestive parallels between various groups of rituals. It is interesting to note further that among the Fijians of the mountainous region of Viti Levu, the installation of the chief is called "Creation of the world," while among the tribes of eastern Vanua Levu it bears the name of *mbuli vanua* or *tuli vanua*, terms which Hocart translates as "fashioning the land" or "creating the earth." [50] For the Scandinavians, as the preceding chapter showed, taking possession of a territory was equivalent to a repetition of the Creation. For the natives of the Fijis, the Creation takes place at each enthronement of a new chief, an idea that is also preserved in other places in more or less obvious forms. Almost everywhere a new reign has been regarded as a regeneration of the history of the people or even of universal history. With each new sovereign, insignificant as he might be, a "new era" began. Such formulas have often been viewed as flattery or stylistic

[49] Trans., XLI (Oxford, 1894), pp. 293, 152. Paul Mus, *Barabudur*, I (Hanoi, 1935), pp. 384 ff.; on "constructed time," II, pp. 733–89.
[50] A. M. Hocart, *Kingship* (London, 1927), pp. 189–90.

artifices. The fact is that they seem exceptional to us only because they have been transmitted to us with a certain solemnity. But in the primitive conception, a new era begins not only with every new reign but also with the consummation of every marriage, the birth of every child, and so on. For the cosmos and man are regenerated ceaselessly and by all kinds of means, the past is destroyed, evils and sins are eliminated, etc. Differing in their formulas, all these instruments of regeneration tend toward the same end: to annul past time, to abolish history by a continuous return *in illo tempore*, by the repetition of the cosmogonic act.

But to return to the Fijians, these islanders repeat the Creation not only on the occasion of each enthronement but also each time that the crops are bad. This detail, upon which Hocart does not insist, since it does not confirm his hypothesis of the "ritual origin" of the cosmogonic myth, seems to us of considerable significance. Each time that life is threatened and the cosmos, in their eyes, is exhausted and empty, the Fijians feel the need for a return *in principio*; in other words they expect the regeneration of cosmic life not from its restoration but from its recreation. Hence the essential importance, in rituals and myths, of anything which can signify the "beginning," the original, the primordial (new vessels and "water drawn before sunrise" in popular magic and medicine, the motifs of the child, the orphan, and so forth).[51]

This idea that life cannot be restored but only re-created through repetition of the cosmogony is very clearly shown in curative rituals. In fact, among many primitive peoples, an essential element of any cure is the recitation of the cosmogonic myth; this is documented, for example, among the most archaic tribes of India, the Bhils, the Santals, the

[51] Cf. our *Comentarii la legenda Meşterului Manole*, especially pp. 56 ff.

Baigas.[52] It is through the actualization of the cosmic Creation, exemplary model of all life, that it is hoped to restore the physical health and spiritual integrity of the patient. Among these tribes the cosmogonic myth is also recited on the occasion of birth, marriage, and death; for it is always through a symbolic return to the atemporal instant of primordial plenitude that it is hoped to assure the perfect realization of each of these situations.

Among the Polynesians, the number of "situations" in which the recitation of the cosmogonic myth is efficacious is still greater. According to the myth, in the beginning there were only the primordial waters, plunged in cosmic darkness. From "within the breathing-space of immensity," Io, the supreme god, expressed the desire to emerge from his repose. Immediately, light appeared. Then he went on: "Ye waters of Tai-Kama, be ye separate. Heavens, be formed!" And thus, through Io's cosmogonic words, the world came into existence. Recalling these "ancient and original sayings . . . the ancient and original cosmological wisdom (*wananga*), which caused growth from the void, etc.," a Polynesian of our day, Hare Hongi, adds, with eloquent awkwardness:

And now, my friends, there are three very important applications of those original sayings, as used in our sacred rituals. The first occurs in the ritual for planting a child in the barren womb. The next occurs in the ritual for enlightening both the mind and body. The third and last occurs in the ritual on the solemn subject of death, and of war, of baptism, of genealogical recitals and such like important subjects, as the priests most particularly concerned themselves in.

The words by which Io fashioned the Universe—that is to say, by which it was implanted and caused to produce a world of light—the same words are used in the ritual for implanting a

[52] Wilhelm Koppers, *Die Bhil in Zentralindien* (Horn, 1948), pp. 241 ff.

child in a barren womb. The words by which Io caused light to shine in the darkness are used in the rituals for cheering a gloomy and despondent heart, the feeble aged, the decrepit; for shedding light into secret places and matters, for inspiration in song-composing and in many other affairs, affecting man to despair in times of adverse war. For all such the ritual includes the words (used by Io) to overcome and dispel darkness. Thirdly, there is the preparatory ritual which treats of successive formations within the universe, and the genealogical history of man himself." [53]

Thus the cosmogonic myth serves the Polynesians as the archetypal model for all "Creations," on whatever plane they are manifested, be it biological, psychological, or spiritual. To listen to the recital of the birth of the world is to become the contemporary of the creative act *par excellence*, the cosmogony. It is significant that among the Navajos the principal occasion for the narration of the cosmogonic myth is in connection with cures. "All the ceremonies center around a patient, Hatrali (one sung over), who may be sick or merely sick in mind, i.e., frightened by a dream, or who may be needing only a ceremony, in order to learn it in the course of being initiated into full power of officiating in that chant—for a Medicine Man cannot give a healing ceremony until he has the ceremony given over him." [54] The ceremony also comprises the execution of complex designs on sand (sand paintings), which symbolize the different stages of the Creation and the mythical history of the gods, the ancestors, and humanity. These designs (which bear a strange resemblance to the Indo-Tibetan *maṇḍalas*) reactualize, one by one, the events which took place *in illo tempore*. Listening to the

---

[53] E. S. C. Handy, *Polynesian Religion* (Honolulu, 1927), pp. 10–11.

[54] Hasteen Klah, *Navajo Creation Myth; The Story of the Emergence* (Mary C. Wheelwright, rec., Navajo Religion Series, I, Museum of Navajo Ceremonial Art, Santa Fe, 1942), p. 19, Cf. also pp. 25 ff., 32 ff.

recital of the cosmogonic myth (followed by the recitation of the myths of origin) and contemplating the sand paintings, the patient is projected out of profane time into the plenitude of primordial time: he has gone back to the origin of the world and is thus a witness of the cosmogony. Very often the patient takes a bath on the same day that the recitation of the myth or the execution of the sand paintings begins; in effect, he too rebegins his life, in the strict sense of the word.

Among the Navajos, as among the Polynesians, the cosmogonic myth is followed by recitation of the myths of origin, which contain the mythical history of all "beginnings": the creation of man, animals, and plants, the origin of the tribe's traditional institutions and culture, and so on. In this way the patient goes over the mythical history of the world, of the Creation, down to the moment when the narrative that is being told was first revealed. This is extremely important for an understanding of primitive and traditional medicine. In the ancient East, as in every "popular" medical tradition, whether in Europe or elsewhere, a remedy becomes effective only if its origin is known and if, consequently, its application becomes contemporary with the mythical moment of its discovery. This is why, in so many incantations, the history of the disease, or of the demon who causes it, is related and at the same time the moment is evoked when a god or a saint succeeded in conquering it. Thus, for example, an Assyrian incantation against toothache relates that "after Anu made the heavens, the heavens made the earth, the earth made the rivers, the rivers made the canals, the canals made the pools, the pools made the Worm." And the Worm goes "weeping" to Shamash and Ea and asks them what will be given it to eat, to "destroy." The gods offer it fruits, but the Worm asks them for human teeth. "Since thou hast

spoken thus, O Worm, may Ea break thee with his powerful hand!" [55] Here we are presented not only with a simple
repetition of the paradigmatic curative gesture (destruction of the Worm by Ea), which ensures the effectiveness
of the treatment, but also with the mythical history of the
disease, by evoking which the doctor projects the patient
in illo tempore.

THE EXAMPLES that we have given could easily be multiplied, but it is not our intention to exhaust the themes we
encounter in this essay; we only wish to situate them in
accordance with a common perspective: the need of archaic
societies to regenerate themselves periodically through the
annulment of time. Collective or individual, periodic or
spontaneous, regeneration rites always comprise, in their
structure and meaning, an element of regeneration through
repetition of an archetypal act, usually of the cosmogonic
act. What is of chief importance to us in these archaic
systems is the abolition of concrete time, and hence their
antihistorical intent. This refusal to preserve the memory
of the past, even of the immediate past, seems to us to
betoken a particular anthropology. We refer to archaic
man's refusal to accept himself as a historical being, his
refusal to grant value to memory and hence to the unusual
events (i.e., events without an archetypal model) that in
fact constitute concrete duration. In the last analysis, what
we discover in all these rites and all these attitudes is the
will to devaluate time. Carried to their extreme, all the
rites and all the behavior patterns that we have so far
mentioned would be comprised in the following statement:
"If we pay no attention to it, time does not exist; furthermore, where it becomes perceptible—because of man's
'sins,' i.e., when man departs from the archetype and

[55] Campbell Thompson, *Assyrian Medical Texts* (London, 1923), p. 59.

falls into duration—time can be annulled." Basically, if viewed in its proper perspective, the life of archaic man (a life reduced to the repetition of archetypal acts, that is, to categories and not to events, to the unceasing rehearsal of the same primordial myths), although it takes place in time, does not bear the burden of time, does not record time's irreversibility; in other words, completely ignores what is especially characteristic and decisive in a consciousness of time. Like the mystic, like the religious man in general, the primitive lives in a continual present. (And it is in this sense that the religious man may be said to be a "primitive"; he repeats the gestures of another and, through this repetition, lives always in an atemporal present.)

That, for a primitive, the regeneration of time is continually effected—that is, *within* the interval of the "year" too—is proven by the antiquity and universality of certain beliefs in respect to the moon. The moon is the first of creatures to die, but also the first to live again. We have elsewhere [56] shown the importance of lunar myths in the organization of the first coherent theories concerning death and resurrection, fertility and regeneration, initiation, and so on. Here it will suffice to recall that, if the moon in fact serves to "measure" time,[57] if the moon's phases—long before the solar year and far more concretely—reveal a unit of time (the month), the moon at the same time reveals the "eternal return."

The phases of the moon—appearance, increase, wane, disappearance, followed by reappearance after three nights of darkness—have played an immense part in the elaboration of cyclical concepts. We find analogous concepts es-

[56] *Patterns in Comparative Religion*, pp. 154 ff.

[57] In the Indo-European languages the majority of terms designating the month and the moon derive from the root *me-*, which, in Latin, in addition to *mensis*, produced *metior*, "to measure."

pecially in the archaic apocalypses and anthropogonies; deluge or flood puts an end to an exhausted and sinful humanity, and a new regenerated humanity is born, usually from a mythical "ancestor" who escaped the catastrophe, or from a lunar animal. A stratigraphic analysis of these groups of myths brings out their lunar character.[58] This means that the lunar rhythm not only reveals short intervals (week, month) but also serves as the archetype for extended durations; in fact, the "birth" of a humanity, its growth, decrepitude ("wear"), and disappearance are assimilated to the lunar cycle. And this assimilation is important not only because it shows us the "lunar" structure of universal becoming but also because of its optimistic consequences: for, just as the disappearance of the moon is never final, since it is necessarily followed by a new moon, the disappearance of man is not final either; in particular, even the disappearance of an entire humanity (deluge, flood, submersion of a continent, and so on) is never total, for a new humanity is born from a pair of survivors.

This cyclical conception of the disappearance and reappearance of humanity is also preserved in the historical cultures. In the third century B.C., Berossus popularized the Chaldean doctrine of the "Great Year" in a form that spread through the entire Hellenic world (whence it later passed to the Romans and the Byzantines). According to this doctrine, the universe is eternal but it is periodically destroyed and reconstituted every Great Year (the corresponding number of millennia varies from school to school); when the seven planets assemble in Cancer ("Great Winter") there will be a deluge; when they meet in Capricorn (i.e., at the summer solstice of the Great Year) the entire universe will be consumed by fire. It is probable that this doctrine of periodic universal conflagra-

[58] Cf. our *Patterns*, Ch. IV.

87

tions was also held by Heraclitus (e.g., Fragment 26B = 66D). In any case, it dominates the thought of Zeno and the entire Stoic cosmology. The myth of universal combustion (*ekpyrosis*) was decidedly in fashion throughout the Romano-Oriental world from the first century B.C. to the third century of our era; it successively found a place in a considerable number of gnostic systems derived from Greco-Irano-Judaic syncretism. Similar ideas (doubtless influenced—at least in their astronomic formulas—by Babylon) are found in India and Iran, as they are among the Mayas of Yucatán and the Aztecs of Mexico. We shall have to return to these questions; but, even now, we are in a position to emphasize what we referred to above as the optimistic character of these ideas. In fact, this optimism can be reduced to a consciousness of the normality of the cyclical catastrophe, to the certainty that it has a meaning and, above all, that it is never final.

In the "lunar perspective," the death of the individual and the *periodic* death of humanity are necessary, even as the three days of darkness preceding the "rebirth" of the moon are necessary. The death of the individual and the death of humanity are alike necessary for their regeneration. Any form whatever, by the mere fact that it exists as such and endures, necessarily loses vigor and becomes worn; to recover vigor, it must be reabsorbed into the formless if only for an instant; it must be restored to the primordial unity from which it issued; in other words, it must return to "chaos" (on the cosmic plane), to "orgy" (on the social plane), to "darkness" (for seed), to "water" (baptism on the human plane, Atlantis on the plane of history, and so on).

We may note that what predominates in all these cosmico-mythological lunar conceptions is the cyclical recurrence of what has been before, in a word, eternal return. Here we again find the motif of the repetition of an archetypal gesture, projected upon all planes—cosmic, biological, historical, human. But we also discover the cyclical structure of time, which is regenerated at each new "birth" on whatever plane. This eternal return reveals an ontology uncontaminated by time and becoming. Just as the Greeks, in their myth of eternal return, sought to satisfy their metaphysical thirst for the "ontic" and the static (for, from the point of view of the infinite, the becoming of things that perpetually revert to the same state is, as a result, implicitly annulled and it can even be affirmed that "the world stands still"),[59] even so the primitive, by conferring a cyclic direction upon time, annuls its irreversibility. Everything begins over again at its commencement every instant. The past is but a prefiguration of the future. No event is irreversible and no transformation is final. In

[59] See Henri-Charles Puech's fine exposition "Gnosis and Time," in *Man and Time* (New York and London, 1957), especially pp. 40–41: "Dominated by an ideal of intelligibility which finds authentic and full being only in that which is in itself and remains identical with itself, in the eternal and immutable, the Greeks regarded movement and change as inferior degrees of reality, in which, at best, identity can be apprehended in the form of permanence and perpetuity, hence of recurrence. The circular movement which assures the survival of the same things by repeating them, by bringing about their continuous return, is the perfect and most immediate expression (hence that which is closest to the divine) of the absolute immobility at the summit of the hierarchy. According to the famous Platonic definition, the time which is determined and measured by the revolution of the celestial spheres is the mobile image of immobile eternity which it imitates by moving in a circle. Consequently both the entire cosmic process and the time of our world of generation and decay develop in a circle or according to an indefinite succession of cycles, in the course of which the same reality is made, unmade, and remade, in conformity with an immutable law and determinate alternations. The same sum of being is preserved; nothing is created and nothing lost; moreover, certain thinkers of dying antiquity—Pythagoreans, Stoics, Platonists—went so far as to maintain that within each of these cycles of time, of these *aiones*, these *aeva*, the same situations recur that have already occurred in the preceding cycles and will occur in subsequent cycles—and so *ad infinitum*. No event is unique, nothing is enacted but once (for example the condemnation of Socrates); every event has been enacted, is enacted, and will be enacted perpetually; the same individuals have appeared, appear, and will appear at every turn of the circle. Cosmic time is repetition and *anakuklosis*, eternal return."

a certain sense, it is even possible to say that nothing new happens in the world, for everything is but the repetition of the same primordial archetypes; this repetition, by actualizing the mythical moment when the archetypal gesture was revealed, constantly maintains the world in the same auroral instant of the beginnings. Time but makes possible the appearance and existence of things. It has no final influence upon their existence, since it is itself constantly regenerated.

Hegel affirmed that in nature things repeat themselves for ever and that there is "nothing new under the sun." All that we have so far demonstrated confirms the existence of a similar conception in the man of archaic societies: for him things repeat themselves for ever and nothing new happens under the sun. But this repetition has a meaning, as we saw in the preceding chapter: it alone confers a reality upon events; events repeat themselves because they imitate an archetype—the exemplary event. Furthermore, through this repetition, time is suspended, or at least its virulence is diminished. But Hegel's observation is significant for another reason: Hegel endeavors to establish a philosophy of history in which the historical event, although irreversible and autonomous, can nevertheless be placed in a dialectic which remains open. For Hegel, history is "free" and always "new," it does not repeat itself; nevertheless, it conforms to the plans of providence; hence it has a model (ideal, but none the less a model) in the dialectic of spirit itself. To this history which does not repeat itself, Hegel opposes nature, in which things are reproduced *ad infinitum*. But we have seen that, during a very considerable period, humanity opposed history by all possible means. May we conclude from all this that, during this period, humanity was still within nature; had not yet detached itself from nature? "Only the animal is truly innocent," Hegel wrote at the beginning of his *Lectures on the Philosophy of History*. The primitives did not always feel themselves innocent, but they tried to return to the state of innocence by periodically confessing their faults. Can we see, in this tendency toward purification, a nostalgia for the lost paradise of animality? Or, in the primitive's desire to have no "memory," not to record time, and to content himself with tolerating it simply as a dimension of his existence, but without "interiorizing" it, without transforming it into consciousness, should we rather see his thirst for the "ontic," his will to be, to *be* after the fashion of the archetypal beings whose gestures he constantly repeats?

The problem is of the first importance, and we certainly cannot hope to discuss it in a few lines. But we have reason to believe that among the primitives the nostalgia for the lost paradise excludes any desire to restore the "paradise of animality." Everything that we know about the mythical memories of "paradise" confronts us, on the contrary, with the image of an ideal humanity enjoying a beatitude and spiritual plenitude forever unrealizable in the present state of "fallen man." In fact, the myths of many peoples allude to a very distant epoch when men knew neither death nor toil nor suffering and had a bountiful supply of food merely for the taking. *In illo tempore*, the gods descended to earth and mingled with men; for their part, men could easily mount to heaven. As the result of a ritual fault, communications between heaven and earth were interrupted and the gods withdrew to the highest heavens. Since then, men must work for their food and are no longer immortal.

Hence it is more probable that the desire felt by the man of traditional societies to refuse history, and to confine himself to an indefinite repetition of archetypes, testifies to his thirst for the real and his terror of "losing" himself by letting himself be overwhelmed by the meaninglessness of profane existence.

It matters little if the formulas and images through which the primitive expresses "reality" seem childish and even absurd to us. It is the profound meaning of primitive behavior that is revelatory; this behavior is governed by belief in an absolute reality opposed to the profane world of "unrealities"; in the last analysis, the latter does not constitute a "world," properly speaking; it is the "unreal" *par excellence*, the uncreated, the nonexistent: the void.

Hence we are justified in speaking of an archaic ontology, and it is only by taking this ontology into consideration that we can succeed in understanding—and hence in not scornfully dismissing—even the most extravagant behavior on the part of the primitive world; in fact, this behavior corresponds to a desperate effort not to lose contact with *being*.

CHAPTER THREE

MISFORTUNE AND HISTORY

*Normality of Suffering · History Regarded as
Theophany · Cosmic Cycles and History
Destiny and History*

*

Normality of Suffering

WITH this chapter, we hope to approach human life and historical existence from a new point of view. Archaic man, as has been shown, tends to set himself in opposition, by every means in his power, to history, regarded as a succession of events that are irreversible, unforeseeable, possessed of autonomous value. He refuses to accept it and to grant it value as such, as *history* —without, however, always being able to exorcise it; for example, he is powerless against cosmic catastrophes, military disasters, social injustices bound up with the very structure of society, personal misfortunes, and so forth. Thus it would be interesting to learn how this "history" was tolerated by archaic man; that is, how he endured the calamities, the mishaps, and the "sufferings" that entered into the lot of each individual and each collectivity.

What does living mean for a man who belongs to a traditional culture? Above all, it means living in accordance with extrahuman models, in conformity with archetypes. Hence it means living at the heart of the *real* since —as Chapter I sufficiently emphasized—there is nothing truly real except the archetypes. Living in conformity with the archetypes amounted to respecting the "law," since the law was only a primordial hierophany, the revelation *in illo tempore* of the norms of existence, a disclosure by a divinity or a mystical being. And if, through the repetition of paradigmatic gestures and by means of periodic ceremonies, archaic man succeeded, as we have seen, in annuling time, he none the less lived in harmony with the cosmic rhythms; we could even say that he entered into these rhythms (we need only remember how "real" night and day are to him, and the seasons, the cycles of the moon, the solstices).

In the frame of such an existence, what could suffering and pain signify? Certainly not a meaningless experience that man can only "tolerate" insofar as it is inevitable, as, for example, he tolerates the rigors of climate. Whatever its nature and whatever its apparent cause, his suffering had a meaning; it corresponded, if not always to a proto-type, at least to an order whose value was not contested. It has been said that one of the great superiorities of Christianity, compared with the old Mediterranean ethics, was that it gave value to suffering: transforming pain from a negative condition to an experience with a positive spiritual content. The assertion is valid insofar as it refers to a giving of value to suffering and even to a seeking out of pain for its salutary qualities. But if pre-Christian humanity did not seek out suffering and did not grant it value (with a few rare exceptions) as an instrument of purifi-cation and spiritual ascent, it was never regarded as mean-ingless. Of course, we here refer to suffering as an event, as a historical fact, to suffering brought on by a cosmic ca-tastrophe (drought, flood, storm), by an invasion (incendi-arism, slavery, humiliation), by social injustices, and so on.

If it was possible to tolerate such sufferings, it is pre-cisely because they seemed neither gratuitous nor arbi-trary. It would be superfluous to cite examples; they are to be found everywhere. The primitive who sees his field laid waste by drought, his cattle decimated by disease, his child ill, himself attacked by fever or too frequently un-lucky as a hunter, knows that all these contingencies are not due to chance but to certain magical or demonic in-fluences, against which the priest or sorcerer possesses weapons. Hence he does as the community does in the case of a catastrophe: he turns to the sorcerer to do away with the magical effect, or to the priest to make the gods favorable to him. If the intervention of priest or sorcerer produces no result, the interested parties recollect the existence of the Supreme Being, who is almost forgotten at other times, and pray to him by offering sacrifices. "Thou who art above, take not my child; he is too young," pray the nomadic Selk'nam of Tierra del Fuego. "O, Tsuni-Goam!" the Hottentots wail. "Thou alone knowest that I am not guilty!" During a storm, the Semang pygmies scratch their calves with bamboo knives and scatter drops of blood in all directions, crying: "Ta Pedn! I am not hardened, I pay for my fault! Accept my debt, I pay it!" [1] We must, in passing, emphasize a point which we developed in detail in our *Patterns in Comparative Religion*: in the cults of the so-called primitive peoples, the celestial Supreme Beings intervene only as the last resort, when every address to gods, demons, and sorcerers, to the end of banishing a suffering (drought, excessive rains, calamity, illness, etc.), has failed. On such an occasion, the Semang pygmies confess the faults of which they believe themselves guilty, a custom which we find sporadically among other peoples, always as an accompaniment to the last recourse to escape from suffering.

Meanwhile, every moment of the magico-religious treatment of suffering most clearly illustrates its meaning: suffering proceeds from the magical action of an enemy, from breaking a taboo, from entering a baneful zone, from the anger of a god, or—when all other hypotheses have proven insufficient—from the will or the wrath of the Supreme Being. The primitive—and not the primitive alone, as we shall see in a moment—cannot conceive of an unprovoked suffering; [2] it arises from a personal fault (if he is con-

[1] See also further examples in Ch. II of our *Patterns in Comparative Religion* (English trans., London and New York, 1958), pp. 46 ff.

[2] We emphasize once again that, from the point of view of anhistorical peoples or classes, "suffering" is equivalent to "history." This equivalence can be observed even today in the peasant civilizations of Europe.

vinced that it is a religious fault) or from his neighbor's malevolence (in cases where the sorcerer discovers that magical action is involved); but there is always a fault at the bottom of it, or at the very least a cause, recognized in the will of the forgotten Supreme God, to whom man is finally forced to address himself. In each case, the suffering becomes intelligible and hence tolerable. Against this suffering, the primitive struggles with all the magico-religious means available to him—but he tolerates it morally because *it is not absurd*. The critical moment of the suffering lies in its appearance; suffering is perturbing only insofar as its cause remains undiscovered. As soon as the sorcerer or the priest discovers what is causing children or animals to die, drought to continue, rain to increase, game to disappear, the suffering begins to become tolerable; it has a meaning and a cause, hence it can be fitted into a system and explained.

What we have just said of the primitive applies in large measure to the man of the archaic cultures. Naturally, the motifs that yield a justification for suffering and pain vary from people to people, but the justification is found everywhere. In general, it may be said that suffering is regarded as the consequence of a deviation in respect to the "norm." That this norm differs from people to people, and from civilization to civilization, goes without saying. But the important point for us is that nowhere—within the frame of the archaic civilizations—are suffering and pain regarded as "blind" and without meaning.

Thus the Indians quite early elaborated a conception of universal causality, the karma concept, which accounts for the actual events and sufferings of the individual's life and at the same time explains the necessity for transmigrations. In the light of the law of karma, sufferings not only find a meaning but also acquire a positive value. The sufferings of one's present life are not only deserved—since they are in fact the fatal effect of crimes and faults committed in previous lives—they are also welcome, for it is only in this way that it is possible to absorb and liquidate part of the karmic debt that burdens the individual and determines the cycle of his future existences. According to the Indian conception, every man is born with a debt, but with freedom to contract new debts. His existence forms a long series of payments and borrowings, the account of which is not always obvious. A man not totally devoid of intelligence can serenely tolerate the sufferings, griefs, and blows that come to him, the injustices of which he is the object, because each of them solves a karmic equation that had remained unsolved in some previous existence. Naturally, Indian speculation very early sought and discovered means through which man can free himself from this endless chain of cause-effect-cause, and so on, determined by the law of karma. But such solutions do nothing to invalidate the meaning of suffering; on the contrary, they strengthen it. Like Yoga, Buddhism sets out from the principle that all existence is pain, and it offers the possibility of a concrete and final way of escape from this unbroken succession of sufferings to which, in the last analysis, every human life can be reduced. But Buddhism, like Yoga, and indeed like every other Indian method of winning liberation, never for a moment casts any doubt upon the "normality" of pain. As to Vedānta, for it suffering is "illusory" only insofar as the whole universe is illusory; neither the human experience of suffering nor the universe is a reality in the ontological sense of the word. With the exception constituted by the materialistic Lokāyata and Chārvāka schools—for which neither the "soul" nor "God" exists and which consider avoiding pain and seeking pleasure the only rational end that man

99

can set himself—all India has accorded to sufferings, whatever their nature (cosmic, psychological, or historical), a clearly defined meaning and function. Karma ensures that everything happening in the world takes place in conformity with the immutable law of cause and effect.

If the archaic world nowhere presents us with a formula as explicit as that of karma to explain the normality of suffering, we do everywhere find in it an equal tendency to grant suffering and historical events a "normal meaning." To treat all the expressions of this tendency here is out of the question. Almost everywhere we come upon the archaic concept (predominant among primitives) according to which suffering is to be imputed to the divine will, whether as directly intervening to produce it or as permitting other forces, demonic or divine, to provoke it. The destruction of a harvest, drought, the sack of a city by an enemy, loss of freedom or life, any calamity (epidemic, earthquake, and so on)—there is nothing that does not, in one way or another, find its explanation and justification in the transcendent, in the divine economy. Whether the god of the conquered city was less powerful than the god of the victorious army; whether a ritual fault, on the part of the entire community or merely on that of a single family, was committed in respect to one divinity or another; whether spells, demons, negligences, curses are involved—an individual or a collective suffering always has its explanation. And, consequently, it is, it *can be*, tolerable.

Nor is this all. In the Mediterranean-Mesopotamian area, man's sufferings were early connected with those of a god. To do so was to endow them with an archetype that gave them both reality and normality. The very ancient myth of the suffering, death, and resurrection of Tammuz has replicas and imitations almost throughout the Paleo-Oriental world, and traces of its scenario were preserved even down to post-Christian gnosticism. This is not the place to enter into the cosmologico-agricultural origins and the eschatological structure of Tammuz. We shall confine ourselves to a reminder that the sufferings and resurrection of Tammuz also provided a model for the sufferings of other divinities (Marduk, for example) and doubtless were mimed (hence repeated) each year by the king. The popular lamentations and rejoicings that commemorated the sufferings, death, and resurrection of Tammuz, or of any other cosmico-agrarian divinity, produced, in the consciousness of the East, a repercussion whose extent has been badly underestimated. For it was not a question merely of a presentiment of the resurrection that will follow death, but also, and no less, of the consoling power of Tammuz' sufferings for each individual. Any suffering could be tolerated if the drama of Tammuz was remembered.

For this mythical drama reminded men that suffering is never final; that death is always followed by resurrection; that every defeat is annulled and transcended by the final victory. The analogy between these myths and the lunar drama outlined in the preceding chapter is obvious. What we wish to emphasize at this point is that Tammuz, or any other variant of the same archetype, justifies—in other words, renders tolerable—the sufferings of the "just." The god—as so often the "just," the "innocent"—suffered without being guilty. He was humiliated, flogged till the lash drew blood, imprisoned in a "pit," that is, in hell. Here it was that the Great Goddess (or, in the later, gnostic versions, a "messenger") visited him, encouraged him, and revived him. This consoling myth of the god's sufferings was long in fading from the consciousness of the peoples of the East. Professor Widengren, for instance, believes that it is among the Manichaean and Mandaean prototypes,[3] though of course with the inevitable changes and new valences that it acquired during the period of Greco-Oriental syncretism. In any case, one fact forces itself upon our attention: such mythological scenarios present an extremely archaic structure, which derives—if not "historically," at least morphologically—from lunar myths whose antiquity we have no reason to question. We have observed that lunar myths afforded an optimistic view of life in general; everything takes place cyclically, death is inevitably followed by resurrection, cataclysm by a new Creation. The paradigmatic myth of Tammuz (also extended to other Mesopotamian divinities) offers us a new ratification of this same optimism: it is not only the individual's death that is "saved"; the same is true of his sufferings. At least the gnostic, Mandaean, and Manichaean echoes of the Tammuz myth suggest this. For these sects, man as such must bear the lot that once fell to Tammuz; fallen into the pit, slave to the Prince of Darkness, man is awakened by a messenger who brings him the good tidings of his imminent salvation, of his "liberation." Lacking though we are in documents that would allow us to extend the same conclusions to Tammuz, we are nevertheless inclined to believe that his drama was not looked upon as foreign to the human drama. Hence the great popular success of rites connected with the so-called vegetation divinities.

History Regarded as Theophany

AMONG the Hebrews, every new historical calamity was regarded as a punishment inflicted by Yahweh, angered by the orgy of sin to which the chosen people had aban-

[3] Geo Widengren, *King and Saviour*, II (Uppsala, 1947).

doned themselves. No military disaster seemed absurd, no suffering was vain, for, beyond the "event," it was always possible to perceive the will of Yahweh. Even more: these catastrophes were, we may say, necessary, they were foreseen by God so that the Jewish people should not contravene its true destiny by alienating the religious heritage left by Moses. Indeed, each time that history gave them the opportunity, each time that they enjoyed a period of comparative peace and economic prosperity, the Hebrews turned from Yahweh and to the Baals and Astartes of their neighbors. Only historical catastrophes brought them back to the right road by forcing them to look toward the true God. Then "they cried unto the Lord, and said, We have sinned, because we have forsaken the Lord, and have served Baalim and Ashtaroth: but now deliver us out of the hand of our enemies, and we will serve thee" (I Samuel 12 : 10). This return to the true God in the hour of disaster reminds us of the desperate gesture of the primitive, who, to rediscover the existence of the Supreme Being, requires the extreme of peril and the failure of all addresses to other divine forms (gods, ancestors, demons). Yet the Hebrews, from the moment the great military Assyro-Babylonian empires appeared on their historical horizon, lived constantly under the threat proclaimed by Yahweh: "But if ye will not obey the voice of the Lord, but rebel against the commandment of the Lord, then shall the hand of the Lord be against you, as it was against your fathers" (I Samuel 12 : 15).

Through their terrifying visions, the prophets but confirmed and amplified Yahweh's ineluctable chastisement upon His people who had not kept the faith. And it is only insofar as such prophecies were ratified by catastrophes (as, indeed, was the case from Elijah to Jeremiah) that historical events acquired religious significance; i.e., that they clearly appeared as punishments inflicted by the Lord in return for the impiousness of Israel. Because of the prophets, who interpreted contemporary events in the light of a strict faith, these events were transformed into "negative theophanies," into Yahweh's "wrath." Thus they not only acquired a meaning (because, as we have seen, for the entire Oriental world, every historical event had its own signification) but they also revealed their hidden coherence by proving to be the concrete expression of the same single divine will. Thus, for the first time, the prophets placed a value on history, succeeded in transcending the traditional vision of the cycle (the conception that ensures all things will be repeated forever), and discovered a one-way time. This discovery was not to be immediately and fully accepted by the consciousness of the entire Jewish people, and the ancient conceptions were still long to survive.

But, for the first time, we find affirmed, and increasingly accepted, the idea that historical events have a value in themselves, insofar as they are determined by the will of God. This God of the Jewish people is no longer an Oriental divinity, creator of archetypal gestures, but a personality who ceaselessly intervenes in history, who reveals his will through events (invasions, sieges, battles, and so on). Historical facts thus become "situations" of man in respect to God, and as such they acquire a religious value that nothing had previously been able to confer on them. It may, then, be said with truth that the Hebrews were the first to discover the meaning of history as the epiphany of God, and this conception, as we should expect, was taken up and amplified by Christianity.

We may even ask ourselves if monotheism, based upon the direct and personal revelation of the divinity, does not necessarily entail the "salvation" of time, its value within the frame of history. Doubtless the idea of revelation is found, in more or less perspicuous form, in all religions, we could even say in all cultures. In fact (the reader may refer to Chapter I), the archetypal gestures—finally reproduced in endless succession by man—were at the same time hierophanies or theophanies. The first dance, the first duel, the first fishing expedition, like the first marriage ceremony or the first ritual, became examples for humanity because they revealed a mode of existence of the divinity, of the primordial man, of the civilizing Hero. But these revelations occurred in *mythical* time, at the extratemporal instant of the beginning; thus, as we saw in Chapter I, everything in a certain sense coincided with the beginning of the world, with the cosmogony. Everything had taken place and had been revealed at that moment, *in illo tempore:* the creation of the world, and that of man, and man's establishment in the situation provided for him in the cosmos, down to the least details of that situation (physiology, sociology, culture, and so on).

The situation is altogether different in the case of the monotheistic revelation. This takes place in time, in historical duration: Moses receives the Law at a certain place and at a certain date. Of course, here too archetypes are involved, in the sense that these events, raised to the rank of examples, will be repeated; but they will not be repeated until the times are accomplished, that is, in a new *illud tempus.* For example, as Isaiah (11 : 15–16) prophesies, the miraculous passages of the Red Sea and the Jordan will be repeated "in the day." Nevertheless, the moment of the revelation made to Moses by God remains a limited moment, definitely situated in time. And, since it also represents a theophany, it thus acquires a new dimension: it becomes precious inasmuch as it is no longer reversible, as it is historical event.

Yet Messianism hardly succeeds in accomplishing the

eschatological valorization of time: the future will regenerate time; that is, will restore its original purity and integrity. Thus, *in illo tempore* is situated not only at the beginning of time but also at its end.[4] In these spacious Messianic visions it is also easy to discern the very old scenario of annual regeneration of the cosmos by repetition of the Creation and by the drama of the suffering king. The Messiah—on a higher plane, of course—assumes the eschatological role of the king as god, or as representing the divinity on earth, whose chief mission was the periodical regeneration of all nature. His sufferings recalled those of the king, but, as in the ancient scenarios, the victory was always finally the king's. The only difference is that this victory over the forces of darkness and chaos no longer occurs regularly every year but is projected into a future and Messianic *illud tempus.*

Under the "pressure of history" and supported by the prophetic and Messianic experience, a new interpretation of historical events dawns among the children of Israel. Without finally renouncing the traditional concept of archetypes and repetitions, Israel attempts to "save" historical events by regarding them as active presences of Yahweh. Whereas, for example, among the Mesopotamian peoples individual or collective sufferings were tolerated insofar as they were caused by the conflict between divine and demonic forces, that is, formed a part of the cosmic drama (the Creation being, from time immemorial and *ad infinitum*, preceded by chaos and tending to be reabsorbed in it; a new birth implying, from time immemorial and *ad infinitum*, sufferings and passions, etc.), in the Israel of the Messianic prophets, historical events could be tolerated because, on the one hand, they were willed

[4] Cf. G. van der Leeuw, "Primordial Time and Final Time," in *Man and Time* (New York and London, 1957), pp. 324–50.

by Yahweh, and, on the other hand, because they were necessary to the final salvation of the chosen people. Rehandling the old scenarios (type: Tammuz) of the "passion" of a god, Messianism gives them a new value, especially by abolishing their possibility of repetition *ad infinitum*. When the Messiah comes, the world will be saved once and for all and history will cease to exist. In this sense we are justified in speaking not only of an eschatological granting of value to the future, to "that day," but also of the "salvation" of historical becoming. History no longer appears as a cycle that repeats itself *ad infinitum*, as the primitive peoples represented it (creation, exhaustion, destruction, annual re-creation of the cosmos), and as it was formulated—as we shall see immediately—in theories of Babylonian origin (creation, destruction, creation extending over considerable periods of time: millennia, Great Years, aeons). Directly ordered by the will of Yahweh, history appears as a series of theophanies, negative or positive, each of which has its intrinsic value. Certainly, all military defeats can be referred back to an archetype: Yahweh's wrath. But each of these defeats, though basically a repetition of the same archetype, nevertheless acquires a coefficient of irreversibility: Yahweh's personal intervention. The fall of Samaria, for example, though assimilable to that of Jerusalem, yet differs from it in the fact that it was provoked by a new gesture on the part of Yahweh, by a new intervention of the Lord in history.

But it must not be forgotten that these Messianic conceptions are the exclusive creation of a religious elite. For many centuries, this elite undertook the religious education of the people of Israel, without always being successful in eradicating the traditional Paleo-Oriental granting of value to life and history. The Hebrews' periodic returns to the Baals and Astartes are also largely to be explained by their refusal to allow a value to history, that is, to regard it as a theophany. For the popular strata, and especially for the agrarian communities, the old religious concept (that of the Baals and Astartes) was preferable; it kept them closer to "life" and helped them to tolerate history if not to ignore it. The Messianic prophets' steadfast will to look history in the face and to accept it as a terrifying dialogue with Yahweh, their will to make military defeats bear moral and religious fruit and to tolerate them because they were regarded as *necessary* to Yahweh's reconciliation with the people of Israel and its final salvation—their will, again, to regard any and every moment as a decisive moment and hence to give it worth religiously —demanded too great a religious tension, and the majority of the Israelites refused to submit to it,[5] just as the majority of Christians, and especially the popular elements, refuse to live the genuine life of Christianity. It was more consoling, and easier, in misfortunes and times of trial, to go on accusing an "accident" (e.g., a spell) or a "negligence" (e.g., a ritual fault) that could easily be made good by a sacrifice (even though it were the sacrifice of infants to Moloch).

In this respect, the classic example of Abraham's sacrifice admirably illustrates the difference between the traditional conception of the repetition of an archetypal gesture

[5] Without religious elites, and more especially without the prophets, Judaism would not have become anything very different from the religion of the Jewish colony in Elephantine, which preserved the popular Palestinian religious viewpoint down to the fifth century B.C.; cf. Albert Vincent, *La Religion des Judéo-Araméens d'Éléphantine* (Paris, 1937). History had allowed these Hebrews of the Diaspora to retain, side by side with Yahweh (Jaho), other divinities (Bethel, Harambethel, Ashumbethel), and even the goddess Anath, in a convenient syncretism. This is one more confirmation of the importance of history in the development of Judaic religious experience and its maintenance under high tensions. For, as we must not forget, the institutions of prophecy and Messianism were above all validated by the pressure of contemporary history.

and the new dimension, *faith*, acquired through religious experience.[6] Morphologically considered, Abraham's sacrifice is nothing but the sacrifice of the first born, a frequent practice in this Paleo-Oriental world in which the Hebrews evolved down to the period of the prophets. The first child was often regarded as the child of a god; indeed, throughout the archaic East, unmarried girls customarily spent a night in the temple and thus conceived by the god (by his representative, the priest, or by his envoy, the "stranger"). The sacrifice of this first child restored to the divinity what belonged to him. Thus the young blood increased the exhausted energy of the god (for the so-called fertility gods exhausted their own substance in the effort expended in maintaining the world and ensuring it abundance; hence they themselves needed to be periodically regenerated). And, in a certain sense, Isaac was a son of God, since he had been given to Abraham and Sarah when Sarah had long passed the age of fertility. But Isaac was given them through their faith; he was the son of the promise and of faith. His sacrifice by Abraham, although in form it resembles all the sacrifices of newborn infants in the Paleo-Semitic world, differs from them fundamentally in content. Whereas, for the entire Paleo-Semitic world, such a sacrifice, despite its religious function, was only a custom, a rite whose meaning was perfectly intelligible, in Abraham's case it is an act of faith. He does not understand why the sacrifice is demanded of him; nevertheless he performs it because it was the Lord who demanded it. By this act, which is apparently absurd, Abraham initiates a

[6] It may be of some service to point out that what is called "faith" in the Judaeo-Christian sense differs, regarded structurally, from other archaic religious experiences. The authenticity and religious validity of these latter must not be doubted, because they are based upon a universally verified dialectic of the sacred. But the experience of faith is due to a new theophany, a new revelation, which, for the respective elites, annuls the validity of other hierophanies. On this subject, see our *Patterns in Comparative Religion*, Ch. I.

new religious experience, faith. All others (the whole Oriental world) continue to move in an economy of the sacred that will be transcended by Abraham and his successors. To employ Kierkegaard's terminology, their sacrifices belonged to the "general"; that is, they were based upon archaic theophanies that were concerned only with the circulation of sacred energy in the cosmos (from the divinity to man and nature, then from man—through sacrifice—back to the divinity, and so on). These were acts whose justification lay in themselves; they entered into a logical and coherent system: what had belonged to God must be returned to him. For Abraham, Isaac was a *gift* from the Lord and not the product of a direct and material conception. Between God and Abraham yawned an abyss; there was a fundamental break in continuity. Abraham's religious act inaugurates a new religious dimension: God reveals himself as personal, as a "totally distinct" existence that ordains, bestows, demands, without any rational (i.e., general and foreseeable) justification, and for which all is possible. This new religious dimension renders "faith" possible in the Judaeo-Christian sense.

We have cited this example in order to illuminate the novelty of the Jewish religion in comparison with the traditional structures. Just as Abraham's experience can be regarded as a new religious position of man in the cosmos, so, through the prophetic office and Messianism, historical events reveal themselves, in the consciousness of the Israelitic elites, as a dimension they had not previously known: the historical event becomes a theophany, in which are revealed not only Yahweh's will but also the personal relations between him and his people. The same conception, enriched through the elaboration of Christology, will serve as the basis for the philosophy of history that Christianity, from St. Augustine on, will labor to construct. But let us repeat: neither in Christianity nor in Judaism does the discovery of this new dimension in religious experience, faith, produce a basic modification of traditional conceptions. Faith is merely made possible for each individual Christian. The great majority of so-called Christian populations continue, down to our day, to preserve themselves from history by ignoring it and by tolerating it rather than by giving it the meaning of a negative or positive theophany.[7]

However, the acceptance and consecration of history by the Judaic elites does not mean that the traditional attitude, which we examined in the preceding chapter, is transcended. Messianic beliefs in a final regeneration of the world themselves also indicate an antihistoric attitude. Since he can no longer ignore or periodically abolish history, the Hebrew tolerates it in the hope that it will finally end, at some more or less distant future moment. The irreversibility of historical events and of time is compensated by the limitation of history to time. In the spiritual horizon of Messianism, resistance to history appears as still more determined than in the traditional horizon of archetypes and repetitions; if, here, history was refused, ignored, or abolished by the periodic repetition of the Creation and by the periodic regeneration of time, in the Messianic conception history must be tolerated because it has an eschatological function, but it can be tolerated only because it is known that, one day or another, it will cease. History is thus abolished, not through consciousness of living an eternal present (coincidence with the atemporal instant of the revelation of archetypes), nor by means of a periodically repeated ritual (for example, the rites for the beginning of the year)—it is abolished in the

---

[7] This does not imply that these populations (which are for the most part agrarian in structure) are nonreligious; it implies only the "traditional" (archetypal) "revalorization" that they have given to Christian experience.

future. Periodic regeneration of the Creation is replaced by a single regeneration that will take place in an *in illo tempore* to come. But the will to put a final and definitive end to history is itself still an antihistorical attitude, exactly as are the other traditional conceptions.

Cosmic Cycles and History

THE MEANING acquired by history in the frame of the various archaic civilizations is nowhere more clearly revealed than in the theories of the great cosmic cycles, which we mentioned in passing in the preceding chapter. We must return to these theories, for it is here that two distinct orientations first define themselves: the one traditional, adumbrated (without ever having been clearly formulated) in all primitive cultures, that of cyclical time, periodically regenerating itself *ad infinitum;* the other modern, that of finite time, a fragment (though itself also cyclical) between two atemporal eternities.

Almost all these theories of the "Great Time" are found in conjunction with the myth of successive ages, the "age of gold" always occurring at the beginning of the cycle, close to the paradigmatic *illud tempus.* In the two doctrines—that of cyclical time, and that of limited cyclical time—this age of gold is recoverable; in other words, it is repeatable, an infinite number of times in the former doctrine, once only in the latter. We do not mention these facts for their intrinsic interest, great as it is, but to clarify the meaning of history from the point of view of either doctrine. We shall begin with the Indian tradition, for it is here that the myth of the eternal return has received its boldest formulation. Belief in the periodic destruction and creation of the universe is already found in the

Atharva-Veda (X, 8, 39–40). The preservation of similar ideas in the Germanic tradition (universal conflagration, Ragnarok, followed by a new creation) confirms the Indo-Aryan structure of the myth, which can therefore be considered one of the numerous variants of the archetype examined in the preceding chapter. (Possible Oriental influences upon Germanic mythology do not necessarily destroy the authenticity and autochthonous character of the Ragnarok myth. It would, besides, be difficult to explain why the Indo-Aryans did not also share, from the period of their common prehistory, the conception of time held by all primitives.)

Indian speculation, however, amplifies and orchestrates the rhythms that govern the periodicity of cosmic creations and destructions. The smallest unit of measure of the cycle is the yuga, the "age." A yuga is preceded and followed by a "dawn" and a "twilight" that connect the ages together. A complete cycle, or Mahāyuga, is composed of four ages of unequal duration, the longest appearing at the beginning of the cycle and the shortest at its end. Thus the first age, the Kṛta Yuga, lasts 4,000 years, plus 400 years of dawn and as many of twilight; then come the Tretā Yuga of 3,000 years, Dvāpara Yuga of 2,000 years, and Kali Yuga of 1,000 years (plus, of course, their corresponding dawns and twilights). Hence a Mahāyuga lasts 12,000 years (*Manu*, I, 69 ff.; *Mahābhārata*, III, 12,826). To the progressive decrease in duration of each new yuga, there corresponds, on the human plane, a decrease in the length of life, accompanied by a corruption in morals and a decline in intelligence. This continuous decadence upon all planes—biological, intellectual, ethical, social, and so on—assumes particular emphasis in the Purāṇic texts (cf., for example *Vayu Purāṇa*, I, 8; *Viṣṇu Purāṇa*, VI, 3). Transition from one yuga to the next takes place, as we have seen, during a twilight, which marks a decrescendo within the yuga itself, each yuga ending by a phase of darkness. As the end of the cycle, that is, the fourth and last yuga, is approached, the darkness deepens. The Kali Yuga, that in which we are today, is, moreover, considered to be the "age of darkness." The complete cycle is terminated by a "dissolution," a Pralaya, which is repeated more intensively (Mahāpralaya, the "great dissolution") at the end of the thousandth cycle.

H. Jacobi [8] rightly believes that, in the original doctrine, a yuga was equivalent to a complete cycle, comprising the birth, "wear," and destruction of the universe. Such a doctrine, moreover, was closer to the archetypal myth (lunar in structure), which we have studied in our *Traité d'histoire des religions*. Later speculation only amplified and reproduced *ad infinitum* the primordial rhythm, creation-destruction-creation, by projecting the unit of measure, the yuga, into more and more extensive cycles. The 12,000 years of a Mahāyuga were considered "divine years," each lasting 360 years, which gives a total of 4,320,000 years for a single cosmic cycle. A thousand such Mahāyuga constitute a Kalpa; fourteen Kalpa make a Manvantāra. A Kalpa is equivalent to a day in the life of Brahmā; another Kalpa to a night. A hundred "years" of Brahmā constitute his life. But even this duration of the life of Brahmā does not succeed in exhausting time, for the gods are not eternal and the cosmic creations and destructions succeed one another *ad infinitum*. (Other systems of calculation even increase the corresponding durations.)

What it is important to note in this avalanche of figures [9]

---

[8] In Hastings' *Encyclopaedia of Religion and Ethics*, I, pp. 200 ff.

[9] Doubtless provoked by the astrological aspect of the yuga, in the establishment of which Babylonian astronomical influences are not excluded; cf. Alfred Jeremias, *Handbuch der altorientalischen Geisteskultur* (2nd edn., Berlin-Leipzig, 1929), p. 303. See also Emil Abegg, *Der Messiasglaube in Indien und Iran* (Berlin,

is the cyclical character of cosmic time. In fact, we are confronted with the infinite repetition of the same phenomenon (creation-destruction-new creation), adumbrated in each yuga (dawn and twilight) but completely realized by a Mahāyuga. The life of Brahmā thus comprises 2,560,-000 of these Mahāyuga, each repeating the same phases (Kṛta, Tretā, Dvāpara, Kali) and ending with a Pralaya, a Ragnarok ("final" destruction, in the sense of a retrogression of all forms to an amorphous mass, occurring at the end of each Kalpa at the time of the Mahāpralaya). In addition to the metaphysical depreciation of history—which, in proportion to and by the mere fact of its duration, provokes an erosion of all forms by exhausting their ontologic substance—and in addition to the myth of the perfection of the beginnings, which we also find here once again, what deserves our attention in this orgy of figures is the eternal repetition of the fundamental rhythm of the cosmos: its periodic destruction and re-creation. From this cycle without beginning or end, man can wrest himself only by an act of spiritual freedom (for all Indian soteriological solutions can be reduced to preliminary liberation from the cosmic illusion and to spiritual freedom).

The two great heterodoxies, Buddhism and Jainism, accept the same pan-Indian doctrine of cyclical time, at least in its chief outlines, and compare it to a wheel with twelve spokes (this image is already employed in Vedic texts; cf. *Atharva-Veda*, X, 8, 4; *Ṛg-Veda*, I, 164, 115; etc.).

As its unit of measure for the cosmic cycles, Buddhism adopts the Kalpa (Pāli: *kappa*), divided into a variable num-

1928), pp. 8 ff.; Isidor Scheftelowitz, *Die Zeit als Schicksalsgottheit in der indischen und iranischen Religion* (Stuttgart, 1929); D. R. Mankad, "Manvantara-Caturyuga Method," *Annals of the Bhandarkar Oriental Research Institute*, XXIII, Silver Jubilee Volume (Poona, 1942), pp. 271–90; and our "Time and Eternity in Indian Thought," in *Man and Time*, pp. 173–200, and in *Images and Symbols: Studies in Religious Symbolism* (English trans., London and New York, 1961), Ch. II.

ber of "incalculables" (asaṃkhyeya, Pāli: asaṇkheyya). Pāli sources generally speak of four asaṇkheyya and a hundred thousand kappa (cf., for example, Jātaka, I, 2); in Mahāyānic literature, the number of incalculables varies between 3, 7, and 33, and they are connected with the career of the Bodhisattva in the various cosmoses.[10] In the Buddhist tradition, the progressive decadence of man is marked by a continuous decrease in the length of human life. Thus, according to Dīgha-nikāya, II, 2–7, at the time of the first Buddha, Vipassi, who made his appearance 91 kappa ago, the length of a human life was 80,000 years; at that of the second Buddha, Sikhi (31 kappa ago), it was 70,000 years, and so on. The seventh Buddha, Gautama, appears when a human life is only 100 years, i.e., has been reduced to the utmost. (We shall encounter the same motif again in Iranian and Christian apocalypses.) Nevertheless, for Buddhism, as for all Indian speculation, time is limitless; and the Bodhisattva will become incarnate to announce the good tidings of salvation to all beings, in aeternum. The only possibility of escaping from time, of breaking the iron circle of existences, is to abolish the human condition and win Nirvana.[11] Besides, all these "incalculables" and all these numberless aeons also have a soteriological function; simply contemplating the panorama of them terrifies man and forces him to realize that

[10] Cf. Asaṇga, Mahāyāna-saṃparigraha, V, 6; Louis de La Vallée-Poussin, Vijñaptimātratāsiddhi (Paris, 1929), pp. 731–33, etc. On calculation of the asaṇkheyya, cf. La Vallée-Poussin's notes in L'Abhidharmakośa (Paris, 1923–1926), III, pp. 188–89; IV, p. 224; and the Mahāprajñāpāramitāśastra of Nāgārjuna, trans. from the Chinese version by Étienne Lamotte, Le Traité de la Grande Vertu de Sagesse de Nāgārjuna, Pt. 1 (Louvain, 1944), pp. 247 ff. On the philosophic conceptions of time, cf. La Vallée-Poussin, "Documents d'Abhidharma: la controverse du temps," Mélanges chinois et bouddhiques, V (Brussels, 1937), pp. 1–158; and Stanislaw Schayer, Contributions to the Problem of Time in Indian Philosophy (Cracow, 1938). Cf. also Mrs. Sinclair Stevenson, The Heart of Jainism (London, 1915), pp. 272 ff.

[11] Cf. our studies, Yoga. Essai sur les origines de la mystique indienne (Paris and Bucharest, 1936), pp. 166 ff.; and Yoga: Immortality and Freedom (English trans., New York and London, 1958), Ch. IV.

he must begin this same transitory existence and endure the same endless sufferings over again, millions upon millions of times; this results in intensifying his will to escape, that is, in impelling him to transcend his condition of "living being," once and for all.

Indian speculations on cyclical time reveal a sufficiently marked "refusal of history." But we must emphasize an aspect in which they differ fundamentally from archaic conceptions; whereas the man of the traditional cultures refuses history through the periodic abolition of the Creation, thus living over and over again in the atemporal instant of the beginnings, the Indian spirit, in its supreme tensions, disparages and even rejects this same reactualization of auroral time, which it no longer regards as an effective solution to the problem of suffering. The difference between the Vedic (hence archaic and primitive) vision and the Mahāyānic vision of the cosmic cycle is, in sum, the very difference that distinguishes the archetypal (traditional) anthropological position from the existentialist (historical) position. Karma, the law of universal causality, which by justifying the human condition and accounting for historical experience could be a source of consolation to the pre-Buddhistic Indian consciousness, becomes, in time, the very symbol of man's "slavery." Hence it is that every Indian metaphysics and technique, insofar as it proposes man's liberation, seeks the annihilation of karma. But if the doctrines of the cosmic cycles had been only an illustration of the theory of universal causality, we should not have mentioned them in the present context. The conception of the four yuga in fact contributes a new element: the explanation (and hence the justification) of historical catastrophes, of the progressive decadence of humanity, biologically, sociologically, ethically, and spiritually. Time, by the simple fact that it is duration, continually aggravates the condition of the cosmos and, by implication, the condition of man. By the simple fact that we are now living in the Kali Yuga, hence in an "age of darkness," which progresses under the sign of disaggregation and must end by a catastrophe, it is our fate to suffer more than the men of preceding ages. Now, in *our* historical moment, we can expect nothing else; at most (and it is here that we glimpse the soteriological function of the Kali Yuga and the privileges conferred on us by a crepuscular and catastrophic history), we can wrest ourselves from cosmic servitude. The Indian theory of the four ages is, consequently, invigorating and consoling for man under the terror of history. In effect: (1) on the one hand, the sufferings that fall to him because he is contemporary with this crepuscular decomposition help him to understand the precariousness of his human condition and thus facilitate his enfranchisement; (2) on the other hand, the theory validates and justifies the sufferings of him who does not choose freedom but resigns himself to undergoing his existence, and this by the very fact that he is conscious of the dramatic and catastrophic structure of the epoch in which it has been given him to live (or, more precisely, to live again).

This second possibility for man to find his place in a "period of darkness," the close of a cycle, is of especial interest to us. It occurs, in fact, in other cultures and at other historical moments. To bear the burden of being contemporary with a disastrous period by becoming conscious of the position it occupies in the descending trajectory of the cosmic cycle is an attitude that was especially to demonstrate its effectiveness in the twilight of Greco-Oriental civilization.

We need not here concern ourselves with the many problems raised by the Orientalo-Hellenistic civilizations.

The only aspect that interests us is the *place* the man of these civilizations finds for himself in respect to history, and more especially as he confronts contemporary history. It is for this reason that we shall not linger over the origin, structure, and evolution of the various cosmological systems in which the antique myth of the cosmic cycles is elaborated and explored, nor over their philosophical consequences. We shall review these cosmological systems— from the pre-Socratics to the Neo-Pythagoreans—only insofar as they answer the following question: What is the meaning of history, that is, of the totality of the human experiences provoked by inevitable geographical conditions, social structures, political conjunctures, and so on? Let us remark at once that this question had meaning only for a very small minority during the period of the Orientalo-Hellenistic civilizations—only for those, that is, who had become dissociated from the horizon of antique spirituality. The immense majority of their contemporaries still lived, especially at the beginning of the period, under the dominance of archetypes; they emerged from it only very late (and perhaps never for good and all, as, for example, in the case of agricultural societies), during the course of the powerful historical tensions that were provoked by Alexander and hardly ended with the fall of Rome. But the philosophical myths and the more or less scientific cosmologies elaborated by this minority, which begins with the pre-Socratics, attained in time to very wide dissemination. What, in the fifth century B.C., was a gnosis accessible only with difficulty, four centuries later becomes a doctrine that consoles hundreds of thousands of men (witness, for example, Neo-Pythagoreanism and Neo-Stoicism in the Roman world). It is, to be sure, through the "success" that they obtained later, and not through their intrinsic worth, that all these Greek and Greco-Oriental doctrines based upon the myth of cosmic cycles are of interest to us.

This myth was still discernibly present in the earliest pre-Socratic speculations. Anaximander knows that all things are born and return to the *apeiron*. Empedocles conceives of the alternate supremacy of the two opposing principles *philia* and *neikos* as explaining the eternal creations and destructions of the cosmos (a cycle in which four phases are distinguishable,[12] somewhat after the fashion of the four "incalculables" of Buddhist doctrine). The universal conflagration is, as we have seen, also accepted by Heraclitus. As to the eternal return—the periodic resumption, by all beings, of their former lives—this is one of the few dogmas of which we know with some certainty that they formed a part of primitive Pythagoreanism.[13] Finally, according to recent researches, admirably utilized and synthesized by Joseph Bidez,[14] it seems increasingly probable that at least certain elements of the Platonic system are of Irano-Babylonian origin.

We shall return to these possible Oriental influences. Let us pause for the moment to consider Plato's interpretation of the myth of cyclical return, more especially in the fundamental text, which occurs in the *Politicus*, 269c ff. Plato finds the cause of cosmic regression and cosmic catastrophes in a twofold motion of the universe: ". . . Of this Universe of ours, the Divinity now guides its circular revolution entirely, now abandons it to itself, once its revolutions have attained the duration which befits this universe; and it then begins to turn in the opposite direction, of its own motion . . ." This change of direction is

---

[12] Cf. Ettore Bignone, *Empedocle* (Turin, 1916), pp. 548 ff.

[13] Dicaearchos, cited by Porphyry, *Vita Pythagorae*, 19.

[14] *Éos, ou Platon et l'Orient* (Brussels, 1945), which takes into consideration especially the researches of Boll, Bezold, W. Gundel, W. Jaeger, A. Götze, J. Stenzel, and even Reitzenstein's interpretations despite the objections that some of them have aroused.

accompanied by gigantic cataclysms: "the greatest destruction, both among animals in general and among the human race, of which, as is fitting, only a few representatives remain" (270c). But this catastrophe is followed by a paradoxical "regeneration." Men begin to grow young again: "the white hair of the aged darkens," while those at the age of puberty begin to lessen in stature day by day, until they return to the size of a new-born infant; then finally, "still continuing to waste away, they wholly cease to be." The bodies of those who died at this time "disappeared completely, without leaving a trace, after a few days" (270e). It was then that the race of the "Sons of Earth" (*gegeneis*), whose memory was preserved by our ancestors, was born (271a). During this age of Cronos, there were neither savage animals nor enmity between animals (271e). The men of those days had neither wives nor children: "Upon arising out of the earth, they all returned to life, without preserving any memory of their former state of life." The trees gave them fruits in abundance and they slept naked on the soil, with no need for beds, because then the seasons were mild (272a).

The myth of the primordial paradise, evoked by Plato, discernible in Indian beliefs, was known to the Hebrews (for example, Messianic *illud tempus* in Isaiah 11 : 6, 8; 65 : 25) as well as to the Iranian (*Dênkart*, VII, 9, 3–5) and Greco-Latin traditions.[15] Moreover, it fits perfectly into the archaic (and probably universal) conception of "paradisal beginnings," which we find in all valuations of the primordial *illud tempus*. That Plato reproduces such traditional visions in the dialogues that date from his old age is nowise astonishing; the evolution of his philosophical thought itself forced him to rediscover the mythological

[15] Cf. Jérôme Carcopino, *Virgile et le mystère de la IVᵉ églogue* (rev. and enl. edn., Paris, 1943), pp. 72 ff.; Franz Cumont, "La Fin du monde selon les mages occidentaux," *Revue de l'Histoire des Religions* (Paris), Jan.–June, 1931, pp. 89 ff.

categories. The memory of the age of gold under Cronos was certainly available to him in Greek tradition (cf., for example, the four ages described by Hesiod, *Erga*, 110 ff.). This fact, however, constitutes no bar to our recognizing that there are also certain Babylonian influences in the *Politicus;* when, for example, Plato imputes periodic cataclysms to planetary revolutions, an explanation that certain recent researches [16] would derive from Babylonian astronomical speculations later rendered accessible to the Hellenic world through Berossus' *Babyloniaca.* According to the *Timaeus*, partial catastrophes are caused by planetary deviation (cf. *Timaeus*, 22d and 23e, deluge referred to by the priest of Saïs), while the moment of the meeting of all the planets is that of "perfect time" (*Timaeus*, 39d), that is, of the end of the Great Year. As Joseph Bidez remarks: "the idea that a conjunction of all the planets suffices to cause a universal upheaval is certainly of Chaldaean origin." [17] On the other hand, Plato seems also to have been familiar with the Iranian conception according to which the purpose of these catastrophes is the purification of the human race (*Timaeus*, 22d).

The Stoics, for their own purposes, also revived speculations concerning the cosmic cycles, emphasizing either eternal repetition [18] or the cataclysm, *ekpyrosis*, by which cosmic cycles come to their end.[19] Drawing from Heraclitus, or directly from Oriental gnosticism, Stoicism propagates all these ideas in regard to the Great Year and to the cosmic fire (*ekpyrosis*) that periodically puts an end to the universe in order to renew it. In time, these motifs of eternal return and of the end of the world come to domi-

[16] Bidez, p. 76.
[17] Ibid., p. 83.
[18] For example, Chrysippus, Fragments 623–27.
[19] As early as Zeno; see Fragments 98 and 109 (H. F. A. von Arnim, *Stoicorum veterum fragmenta*, I, Leipzig, 1921).

nate the entire Greco-Roman culture. The periodic renewal of the world (*metacosmesis*) was, furthermore, a favorite doctrine of Neo-Pythagoreanism, the philosophy that as Jérôme Carcopino has shown, together with Stoicism, divided the allegiance of Roman society in the second and first centuries B.C. But adherence to the myth of "eternal repetition," as well as to that of *apokatastasis* (the term entered the Hellenic world after Alexander the Great) are both philosophical positions in which we can perceive a very determined antihistorical attitude together with a will to defend oneself from history. We shall discuss both of these positions.

We observed in the preceding chapter that the myth of eternal repetition, as reinterpreted by Greek speculation, has the meaning of a supreme attempt toward the "static-ization" of becoming, toward annulling the irreversibility of time. If all moments and all situations of the cosmos are repeated *ad infinitum*, their evanescence is, in the last analysis, patent; *sub specie infinitatis*, all moments and all situations remain stationary and thus acquire the ontological order of the archetype. Hence, among all the forms of becoming, historical becoming too is saturated with being. From the point of view of eternal repetition, historical events are transformed into categories and thus regain the ontological order they possessed in the horizon of archaic spirituality. In a certain sense it can even be said that the Greek theory of eternal return is the final variant undergone by the myth of the repetition of an archetypal gesture, just as the Platonic doctrine of Ideas was the final version of the archetype concept, and the most fully elaborated. And it is worth noting that these two doctrines found their most perfect expression at the height of Greek philosophical thought.

But it was especially the myth of universal conflagration

123

that achieved a marked success throughout the Greco-Oriental world. It appears more and more probable that the myth of an end of the world by fire, from which the good will escape unharmed, is of Iranian origin (cf., for example, *Bundahišn*, XXX, 18), at least in the form known to the "western mages" who, as Cumont has shown,[20] disseminated it in the West. Stoicism, the *Sibylline Oracles* (for example II, 253), and Judaeo-Christian literature make this myth the foundation of their apocalypses and their eschatology. Strange as it may seem, the myth was consoling. In fact, fire renews the world; through it will come the restoration of "a new world, free from old age, death, decomposition and corruption, living eternally, increasing eternally, when the dead shall rise, when immortality shall come to the living, when the world shall be perfectly renewed" (*Yašt*, XIX, 14, 89).[21] This, then, is an *apokatastasis* from which the good have nothing to fear. The final catastrophe will put an end to history, hence will restore man to eternity and beatitude.

Notable studies, by both Cumont and H. S. Nyberg,[22] have succeeded in illuminating some of the obscurity that surrounds Iranian eschatology and in defining the influences responsible for the Judaeo-Christian apocalypse. Like India (and, in a certain sense, Greece), Iran knew the myth of the four cosmic ages. A lost Mazdean text, the *Sudkar-nask* (whose content is preserved in the *Dênkart*, IX, 8), referred to the four ages: gold, silver, steel, and

[20] Op. cit., pp. 39 ff.

[21] After James Darmesteter's trans. in *Le Zend-Avesta* (Paris, 1892).

[22] Cf. Nyberg's "Questions de cosmogonie et de cosmologie mazdéennes," *Journal Asiatique* (Paris), CCXIV, CCXIX (1929, 1931). See also Scheftelowitz, op. cit.; R. C. Zaehner, "Zurvanica," *Bulletin of the School of Oriental and African Studies* (London), IX (1937–39), 303 ff., 573 ff., 871 ff.; H. H. Schaeder, "Der iranische Zeitgott und sein Mythos," *Zeitschrift der Deutschen Morgenländischen Gesellschaft* (Leipzig), XCV (1941), 268 ff.; Henry Corbin, "Cyclical Time in Mazdaism and Ismailism," in *Man and Time*, especially pp. 121 ff.

"mixed with iron." The same metals are mentioned at the beginning of the *Bahman-Yašt* (I, 3), which, however, somewhat further on (II, 14), describes a cosmic tree with seven branches (gold, silver, bronze, copper, tin, steel, and a "mixture of iron"), corresponding to the sevenfold mythical history of the Persians.[23] This cosmic hebdomad no doubt developed in connection with Chaldaean astrological teachings, each planet "governing" a millennium. But Mazdaism had much earlier proposed an age of 9,000 years (3 × 3,000) for the universe, while Zarvanism, as Nyberg has shown,[24] extended the maximum duration of this universe to 12,000 years. In the two Iranian systems—as, moreover, in all doctrines of cosmic cycles—the world will end by fire and water, *per pyrosim et cataclysmum*, as Firmicus Maternus (III, 1) was later to write. That in the Zarvanite system "unlimited time," *Zarvan akarana*, precedes and follows the 12,000 years of "limited time" created by Ormazd; that in this system "Time is more powerful than the two Creations,"[25] that is, than the creations of Ormazd and Ahriman; that, consequently, *Zarvan akarana* was not created by Ormazd and hence is not subordinate to him—all these are matters that we need not enter into here. What we wish to emphasize is that, in the Iranian conception, history (whether followed or not by infinite time) is not eternal; it does not repeat itself but will come to an end one day by an eschatological *ekpyrosis* and cosmic cataclysm. For the final catastrophe that will put an end to history will at the same time be a judgment of history. It is then—*in illo tempore*—that, as we are told, all will render an account of what they have

[23] Cf. Cumont, op. cit., pp. 71 ff.
[24] Op. cit., pp. 41 ff., 235.
[25] *Bundahišn*, Ch. I (Nyberg, pp. 214–15).

done "in history" and only those who are not guilty will know beatitude and eternity.[26]

Windisch has shown the importance of these Mazdean ideas for the Christian apologist Lactantius.[27] God created the world in six days, and on the seventh he rested; hence the world will endure for six aeons, during which "evil will conquer and triumph" on earth. During the seventh millennium, the prince of demons will be chained and humanity will know a thousand years of rest and perfect justice. After this the demon will escape from his chains and resume war upon the just; but at last he will be vanquished and at the end of the eighth millennium the world will be re-created for eternity. Obviously, this division of history into three acts and eight millennia was also known to the Christian chiliasts,[28] but there can be no doubt that it is Iranian in structure, even if a similar eschatological vision of history was disseminated throughout the Mediterranean East and in the Roman Empire by Greco-Oriental gnosticisms.

A series of calamities will announce the approach of the end of the world; and the first of them will be the fall of Rome and the destruction of the Roman Empire, a frequent anticipation in the Judaeo-Christian apocalypse, but also not unknown to the Iranians.[29] The apocalyptic syndrome is, furthermore, common to all these traditions. Both Lactantius and the *Bahman-Yašt* announce that "the year will be shortened, the month will diminish, and the day will contract,"[30] a vision of cosmic and human deterioration that we have also found in India (where human life decreases from 80,000 to 100 years) and that astrologi-

[26] The Oriental and Judaeo-Christian symbolism of passing through fire has recently been studied by C. M. Edsman, *Le Baptême de feu* (Uppsala, 1940).

[27] Cf. Cumont, pp. 68 ff.

[28] Ibid., p. 70, note 5.

[29] Ibid., p. 72.

[30] Texts in ibid., p. 78, note 1.

cal doctrines popularized in the Greco-Oriental world. Then the mountains will crumble and the earth become smooth, men will desire death and envy the dead, and but a tenth of them will survive. "It will be a time," writes Lactantius, "when justice will be rejected and innocence odious, when the wicked will prey as enemies upon the good, when neither law nor order nor military discipline will be observed, when none will respect gray hairs, or do the offices of piety, nor take pity upon women and children; all things will be confounded and mixed, against divine and natural law. . . ." [31] But after this premonitory phase, the purifying fire will come down to destroy the wicked and will be followed by the millennium of bliss that the Christian chiliasts also expected and Isaiah and the *Sibylline Oracles* had earlier foretold. Men will know a new golden age that will last until the end of the seventh millennium; for after this last conflict, a universal *ekpyrosis* will absorb the whole universe in fire, thus permitting the birth of a new world, an eternal world of justice and happiness, not subject to astral influences and freed from the dominion of time.

The Hebrews likewise limited the duration of the world to seven millennia,[32] but the rabbinate never encouraged mathematical calculations to determine the end of the world. They confined themselves to stating that a series of cosmic and historical calamities (famines, droughts, wars, and so forth) would announce the end of the world. The Messiah would come; the dead would rise again (Isaiah 26 : 19); God would conquer death and the renewal of the world would follow (Isaiah 65 : 17; Book of Jubilees I : 29, even speaks of a new Creation).[33]

[31] *Divinae Institutiones*, VII, 17, 9; Cumont, p. 81.

[32] Cf., for example, *Testamentum Abrahami, Ethica Enochi*, etc.

[33] On cosmic signs presaging the Messiah in rabbinical literature, see Raphael Patai, *Man and Temple* (London, 1947), pp. 203 ff.

Here again, as everywhere in the apocalyptic doctrines referred to above, we find the traditional motif of extreme decadence, of the triumph of evil and darkness, which precede the change of aeon and the renewal of the cosmos. A Babylonian text translated by A. Jeremias [34] thus foresees the apocalypse: "When such and such things happen in heaven, then will the clear become dull, the pure dirty, the lands will fall into confusion, prayers will not be heard, the signs of the prophets will become unfavorable. . . . Under his [i.e., a prince who does not obey the commands of the gods] rule the one will devour the other, the people will sell their children for gold, the husband will desert his wife, the wife her husband, the mother will bolt the door against her daughter." Another hymn foretells that, in those days, the sun will no longer rise, the moon no longer appear, and so on.

In the Babylonian conception, however, this crepuscular period is always followed by a new paradisal dawn. Frequently, as we should expect, the paradisal period opens with the enthronement of a new sovereign. Ashurbanipal regards himself as a regenerator of the cosmos, for "since the time the gods in their friendliness did set me on the throne of my fathers, Ramman has sent forth his rain . . . the harvest was plentiful, the corn was abundant . . . the cattle multiplied exceedingly." Nebuchadrezzar says of himself: "A reign of abundance, years of exuberance in my country I cause to be." In a Hittite text, Murshilish thus describes the reign of his father: ". . . under him the whole land of Katti prospered, and in his time people, cattle, sheep multiplied." [35] The conception is archaic and

---

[34] Hastings, I, p. 187.
[35] Ivan Engnell, *Studies in Divine Kingship in the Ancient Near East* (Uppsala, 1943), pp. 43, 44, 68; Jeremias, *Handbuch*, pp. 32 ff.

universal: we find it in Homer, in Hesiod, in the Old Testament, in China, and elsewhere.[36]

Simplifying, we might say that, among the Iranians as among the Jews and Christians, the "history" apportioned to the universe is limited, and that the end of the world coincides with the destruction of sinners, the resurrection of the dead, and the victory of eternity over time. But although this doctrine becomes increasingly popular during the first century B.C. and the early centuries of our era, it does not succeed in finally doing away with the traditional doctrine of periodic regeneration of the world through annual repetition of the Creation. We saw in the preceding chapter that vestiges of this latter doctrine were preserved among the Iranians until far into the Middle Ages. Similarly dominant in pre-Messianic Judaism, it was never totally eliminated, for rabbinic circles hesitated to be precise as to the duration that God had fixed for the cosmos and confined themselves to declaring that the *illud tempus* would certainly arrive one day. In Christianity, on the other hand, the evangelical tradition itself implies that βασίλεια τοῦ θεοῦ is already present "among" (ἐντός) those who believe, and that hence the *illud tempus* is eternally of the present and accessible to anyone, at any moment, through *metanoia*. Since what is involved is a religious experience wholly different from the traditional experience, since what is involved is faith, Christianity translates the periodic regeneration of the world into a regeneration of the human individual. But for him who shares in this eternal *nunc* of the reign of God, history ceases as totally as it does for the man of the archaic cultures, who abolishes it periodically. Consequently, for the

[36] *Odyssey*, XIX, 108 ff.; Hesiod, *Erga*, 225–27; our *Patterns in Comparative Religion*, pp. 255 ff.; Patai, p. 180 (rabbinical literature); Léon Wieger, *Histoire des croyances religieuses et des opinions philosophiques en Chine* (Hsien-hsien, 1922), p. 64.

Christian too, history can be regenerated, by and through each individual believer, even before the Saviour's second coming, when it will utterly cease for all Creation.

An adequate discussion of the revolution that Christianity introduced into the dialectic of the abolition of history, and of the escape from the ascendancy of time, would lead us too far beyond the limits of this essay. Let us simply note that even within the frame of the three great religious—Iranian, Judaic, and Christian—that have limited the duration of the cosmos to some specific number of millennia and affirm that history will finally cease *in illo tempore*, there still survive certain traces of the ancient doctrine of the periodic regeneration of history. In other words, history can be abolished, and consequently renewed, a number of times, before the final *eschaton* is realized. Indeed, the Christian liturgical year is based upon a periodic and real repetition of the Nativity, Passion, death, and Resurrection of Jesus, with all that this mystical drama implies for a Christian; that is, personal and cosmic regeneration through reactualization *in concreto* of the birth, death, and resurrection of the Saviour.

Destiny and History

WE HAVE referred to all these Hellenistic-Oriental doctrines relative to cosmic cycles for only one purpose—that of discovering the answer to the question that we posed at the beginning of this chapter: How has man tolerated history? The answer is discernible in each individual system: His very place in the cosmic cycle—whether the cycle be capable of repetition or not—lays upon man a certain historical destiny. We must beware of seeing no more here than a fatalism, whatever meaning we ascribe to the term,

130

that would account for the good and bad fortune of each individual taken separately. These doctrines answer the questions posed by the destiny of contemporary history in its entirety, not only those posed by the individual destiny. A certain quantity of suffering is in store for humanity (and by the word "humanity" each person means the mass of men known to himself) by the simple fact that humanity finds itself at a certain historical moment, that is, in a cosmic cycle that is in its descending phase or nearing its end. Individually, each is free to withdraw from this historical moment and to console himself for its baneful consequences, whether through philosophy or through mysticism. (The mere mention of the swarm of gnosticisms, sects, mysteries, and philosophies that overran the Mediterranean-Oriental world during the centuries of historical tension will suffice to give an idea of the vastly increasing proportion of those who attempted to withdraw from history.) The historical moment in its totality, however, could not avoid the destiny that was the inevitable consequence of its very position upon the descending trajectory of the cycle to which it belonged. Just as, in the Indian view, every man of the Kali Yuga is stimulated to seek his freedom and spiritual beatitude, yet at the same time cannot avoid the final dissolution of this crepuscular world in its entirety, so, in the view of the various systems to which we have referred, the historical moment, despite the possibilities of escape it offers contemporaries, can never, in its entirety, be anything but tragic, pathetic, unjust, chaotic, as any moment that heralds the final catastrophe must be.

In fact, a common characteristic relates all the cyclical systems scattered through the Hellenistic-Oriental world: in the view of each of them, the contemporary historical moment (whatever its chronological position) represents a decadence in relation to preceding historical moments. Not only is the contemporary aeon inferior to the other ages (gold, silver, and so on) but, even within the frame of the reigning age (that is, of the reigning cycle), the "instant" in which man lives grows worse as time passes. This tendency toward devaluation of the contemporary moment should not be regarded as a sign of pessimism. On the contrary, it reveals an excess of optimism, for, in the deterioration of the contemporary situation, at least a portion of mankind saw signs foretelling the regeneration that must necessarily follow. Since the days of Isaiah, a series of military defeats and political collapses had been anxiously awaited as an ineluctable syndrome of the Messianic *illud tempus* that was to regenerate the world.

However, different as were the possible positions of man, they displayed one common characteristic: history could be tolerated, not only because it had a meaning but also because it was, in the last analysis, necessary. For those who believed in a repetition of an entire cosmic cycle, as for those who believed only in a single cycle nearing its end, the drama of contemporary history was necessary and inevitable. Plato, even in his day, and despite his acceptance of some of the schemata of Chaldaean astrology, was profuse in his sarcasms against those who had fallen into astrological fatalism or who believed in an eternal repetition in the strict (Stoic) sense of the term (cf., for example, *Republic*, VIII, 546 ff.). As for the Christian philosophers, they fiercely combated the same astrological fatalism,[37] which had increased during the last

---

[37] Among many other liberations, Christianity effected liberation from astral destiny: "We are above Fate," Tatian writes (*Oratio ad Graecos*, 9), summing up Christian doctrine. "The sun and the moon were made for us; how am I to worship what are my servitors " (ibid., 4). Cf. also St. Augustine, *De civitate Dei*, XII, Ch. X–XIII; on the ideas of St. Basil, Origen, St. Gregory, and St. Augustine, and their opposition to cyclical theories, see Pierre Duhem, *Le Système du monde* (Paris, 1913–17), II, pp. 446 ff. See also Henri-Charles Puech, "Gnosis and Time," in *Man and Time*, pp. 38 ff.

centuries of the Roman Empire. As we shall see in a moment, Saint Augustine will defend the idea of a perennial Rome solely to escape from accepting a *fatum* determined by cyclical theories. It is, nevertheless, true that astrological fatalism itself accounted for the course of historical events, and hence helped the contemporary to understand them and tolerate them, just as successfully as did the various Greco-Oriental gnosticisms, Neo-Stoicism, and Neo-Pythagoreanism. For example, whether history was governed by the movements of the heavenly bodies or purely and simply by the cosmic process, which necessarily demanded a disintegration inevitably linked to an original integration, whether, again, it was subject to the will of God, a will that the prophets had been able to glimpse, the result was the same: none of the catastrophes manifested in history was arbitrary. Empires rose and fell; wars caused innumerable sufferings; immorality, dissoluteness, social injustice, steadily increased—because all this was necessary, that is, was willed by the cosmic rhythm, by the demiurge, by the constellations, or by the will of God.

In this view, the history of Rome takes on a noble gravity. Several times in the course of their history, the Romans underwent the terror of an imminent end to their city, whose duration—as they believed—had been determined at the very moment of its foundation by Romulus. In *Les Grands Mythes de Rome*, Jean Hubaux has penetratingly analyzed the critical moments of the drama provoked by the uncertainties in calculations of the "life" of Rome, while Jérôme Carcopino has recorded the historical events and the spiritual tension that justified the hope for a noncatastrophic resurrection of the city.[38] At every historical crisis two crepuscular myths obsessed the Roman people: (1) the life of the city is ended, its duration being limited to a certain number of years (the "mystic number"

[38] Jean Hubaux, *Les Grands Mythes de Rome* (Paris, 1945); Carcopino, op. cit.

revealed by the twelve eagles seen by Romulus); and (2) the Great Year will put an end to all history, hence to that of Rome, by a universal *ekpyrosis*. Roman history itself undertook to show the baselessness of these fears, down to a very late period. For at the end of 120 years after the foundation of Rome, it was realized that the twelve eagles seen by Romulus did not signify 120 years of historical life for the city, as many had feared. At the end of 365 years, it became apparent that there was no question of a Great Year, in which each year of the city would be equivalent to a day, and it was supposed that destiny had granted Rome another kind of Great Year, composed of twelve months of 100 years. As for the myth of regressive "ages" and eternal return, professed by the Sibyl and interpreted by the philosophers through their theories of cosmic cycles, it was more than once hoped that the transition from one age to the other could be effected without a universal *ekpyrosis*. But this hope was always mingled with anxiety. Each time historical events accentuated their catastrophic rhythm, the Romans believed that the Great Year was on the point of ending and that Rome was on the eve of her fall. When Caesar crossed the Rubicon, Nigidius Figulus foresaw the beginning of a cosmico-historical drama which would put an end to Rome and the human race.[39] But the same Nigidius Figulus believed [40] that an *ekpyrosis* was not inevitable, and that a renewal, the Neo-Pythagorean *metacosmesis*, was also possible without a cosmic catastrophe— an idea that Virgil was to take up and elaborate.

Horace, in his *Epode XVI*, had been unable to conceal his fear as to the future fate of Rome. The Stoics, the astrologers, and Oriental gnosticism saw in the wars and calamities of the time signs that the final catastrophe was

[39] Lucan, *Pharsalia*, 639, 642–45; Carcopino, p. 147.
[40] Ibid., pp. 52 ff.

imminent. Reasoning either from calculation of the life of Rome or from the doctrine of cosmico-historical cycles, the Romans knew that, whatever else might happen, the city was fated to disappear before the beginning of a new aeon. But the reign of Augustus, coming after a series of long and sanguinary civil wars, seemed to inaugurate a *pax aeterna*. The fears inspired by the two myths—the "age" of Rome and the theory of the Great Year—now proved groundless: "Augustus has founded Rome anew and we have nothing to fear as to its life," those who had been concerned over the mystery of Romulus' twelve eagles could assure themselves. "The transition from the age of iron to the age of gold has been accomplished without an *ekpyrosis*," those who had been obsessed by the theory of cycles could say. Thus Virgil, for the last *saeculum*, that of the sun, which was to bring about the combustion of the universe, could substitute the *saeculum* of Apollo, avoiding an *ekpyrosis* and assuming that the recent wars had themselves been the sign of the transition from the age of iron to the age of gold.[41] Later, when Augustus' reign seemed indeed to have inaugurated the age of gold, Virgil undertook to reassure the Romans as to the duration of the city. In the *Aeneid* (I, 255 ff.) Jupiter, addressing Venus, assures her that he will lay no bounds of space or time upon the Romans: "empire without end have I given them."[42] And it was not until after the publication of the *Aeneid* that Rome was called *urbs aeterna*, Augustus being proclaimed the second founder of the city. His birthday, September 23, was regarded "as the point of departure of the Universe, whose existence had been saved, and whose face had been changed, by Augustus."[43] Then arose the hope that Rome

[41] Cf. ibid., p. 45, etc.
[42] "His ego nec metas rerum nec tempora pono: imperium sine fine dedi"; cf. Hubaux, p. 128 ff.
[43] Carcopino, p. 200.

could regenerate itself periodically *ad infinitum.* Thus it was that, liberated from the myths of the twelve eagles and of the *ekpyrosis*, Rome could increase until, as Virgil foretells, it embraced even the regions "beyond the paths of the sun and the year" ("extra anni solisque vias").

In all this, as we see, there is a supreme effort to liberate history from astral destiny or from the law of cosmic cycles and to return, through the myth of the eternal renewal of Rome, to the archaic myth of the annual (and in particular the noncatastrophic!) regeneration of the cosmos through its eternal re-creation by the sovereign or the priest. It is above all an attempt to give value to history on the cosmic plane; that is, to regard historical events and catastrophes as genuine cosmic combustions or dissolutions that must periodically put an end to the universe in order to permit its regeneration. The wars, the destruction, the sufferings of history are no longer the premonitory signs of the transition from one age to another, but themselves constitute the transition. Thus in each period of peace, history renews itself and, consequently, a new world begins; in the last analysis (as we saw in the case of the myth built up around Augustus), the sovereign repeats the Creation of the cosmos.

We have adduced the example of Rome to show how historical events could be given value by the expedient of the myths examined in the present chapter. Adapted to a particular myth theory (age of Rome, Great Year), catastrophes could not only be tolerated by their contemporaries but also *positively* accorded a value immediately after their appearance. Of course, the age of gold inaugurated by Augustus has survived only through what it created in Latin culture. Augustus was no sooner dead than history undertook to belie the age of gold, and once again people began living in expectation of imminent disaster. When

Rome was occupied by Alaric, it seemed that the sign of Romulus' twelve eagles had triumphed: the city was entering its twelfth and last century of existence. Only Saint Augustine attempted to show that no one could know the moment at which God would decide to put an end to history, and that in any case, although cities by their very nature have a limited duration, the only "eternal city" being that of God, no astral destiny can decide the life or death of a nation. Thus Christian thought tended to transcend, once and for all, the old themes of eternal repetition, just as it had undertaken to transcend all the other archaic viewpoints by revealing the importance of the religious experience of faith and that of the value of the human personality.

CHAPTER FOUR

THE TERROR OF HISTORY

*Survival of the Myth of Eternal Return · The
Difficulties of Historicism · Freedom and
History · Despair or Faith*

*

Survival of the Myth of Eternal Return

THE problem raised in this final chapter exceeds the limits that we had assigned to the present essay. Hence we can only outline it. In short, it would be necessary to confront "historical man" (modern man), who consciously and voluntarily creates history, with the man of the traditional civilizations, who, as we have seen, had a negative attitude toward history. Whether he abolishes it periodically, whether he devaluates it by perpetually finding transhistorical models and archetypes for it, whether, finally, he gives it a metahistorical meaning (cyclical theory, eschatological significations, and so on), the man of the traditional civilizations accorded the historical event no value in itself; in other words, he did not regard it as a specific category of his own mode of existence. Now, to compare these two types of humanity implies an analysis of all the modern "historicisms," and such an analysis, to be really useful, would carry us too far from the principal theme of this study. We are nevertheless forced to touch upon the problem of man as consciously and voluntarily historical, because the modern world is, at the present moment, not entirely converted to historicism; we are even witnessing a conflict between the two views: the archaic conception, which we should designate as archetypal and anhistorical; and the modern, post-Hegelian conception, which seeks to be historical. We shall confine ourselves to examining only one aspect of the problem, but an important aspect: the solutions offered by the historicistic view to enable modern man to tolerate the increasingly powerful pressure of contemporary history.

The foregoing chapters have abundantly illustrated the way in which men of the traditional civilizations tolerated history. The reader will remember that they defended themselves against it, either by periodically abolishing it through repetition of the cosmogony and a periodic regeneration of time or by giving historical events a metahistorical meaning, a meaning that was not only consoling but was above all coherent, that is, capable of being fitted into a well-consolidated system in which the cosmos and man's existence had each its *raison d'être*. We must add that this traditional conception of a defense against history, this way of tolerating historical events, continued to prevail in the world down to a time very close to our own; and that it still continues to console the agricultural (= traditional) societies of Europe, which obstinately adhere to an anhistorical position and are, by that fact, exposed to the violent attacks of all revolutionary ideologies. The Christianity of the popular European strata never succeeded in abolishing either the theory of the archetype (which transformed a historical personage into an exemplary hero and a historical event into a mythical category) or the cyclical and astral theories (according to which history was justified, and the sufferings provoked by it assumed an eschatological meaning). Thus—to give only a few examples—the barbarian invaders of the High Middle Ages were assimilated to the Biblical archetype Gog and Magog and thus received an ontological status and an eschatological function. A few centuries later, Christians were to regard Genghis Khan as a new David, destined to accomplish the prophecies of Ezekiel. Thus interpreted, the sufferings and catastrophes provoked by the appearance of the barbarians on the medieval historical horizon were "tolerated" by the same process that, some thousands of years earlier, had made it possible to tolerate the terrors of history in the ancient East. It is such justifications of historical catastrophes that today still make life possible for tens of millions of men, who continue to recognize, in the unremitting pressure of events, signs of the divine will or of an astral fatality.

If we turn to the other traditional conception—that of cyclical time and the periodic regeneration of history, whether or not it involves the myth of eternal repetition— we find that, although the earliest Christian writers began by violently opposing it, it nevertheless in the end made its way into Christian philosophy. We must remind ourselves that, for Christianity, time is real because it has a meaning—the Redemption. "A straight line traces the course of humanity from initial Fall to final Redemption. And the meaning of this history is unique, because the Incarnation is a unique fact. Indeed, as Chapter 9 of the Epistle to the Hebrews and I Peter 3 : 18 emphasize, Christ died for our sins once only, once for all (*hapax*, *ephapax*, *semel*); it is not an event subject to repetition, which can be reproduced several times (*pollakis*). The development of history is thus governed and oriented by a unique fact, a fact that stands entirely alone. Consequently the destiny of all mankind, together with the individual destiny of each one of us, are both likewise played out once, once for all, in a concrete and irreplaceable time which is that of history and life." [1] It is this linear conception of time and history, which, already outlined in the second century by St. Irenaeus of Lyon, will be taken up again by St. Basil and St. Gregory and be finally elaborated by St. Augustine.

But despite the reaction of the orthodox Fathers, the theories of cycles and of astral influences on human destiny and historical events were accepted, at least in part, by

[1] Henri-Charles Puech, "Gnosis and Time," in *Man and Time* (New York and London, 1957), pp. 48 ff. Cf. also the same author's "Temps, histoire et mythe dans le christianisme des premiers siècles," *Proceedings of the VIIth Congress for the History of Religion* (Amsterdam, 1951), pp. 33–52.

other Fathers and ecclesiastical writers, such as Clement of Alexandria, Minucius Felix, Arnobius, and Theodoret. The conflict between these two fundamental conceptions of time and history continued into the seventeenth century. We cannot even consider recapitulating the admirable analyses made by Pierre Duhem and Lynn Thorndike, and resumed and completed by Pitirim Sorokin.[2] We must remind the reader that, at the height of the Middle Ages, cyclical and astral theories begin to dominate historiological and eschatological speculation. Already popular in the twelfth century,[3] they undergo systematic elaboration in the next, especially after the appearance of translations from Arabic writers.[4] Increasingly precise correlations are attempted between the cosmic and the geographical factors involved and the respective periodicities (in the direction already indicated by Ptolemy, in the second century of our era, in his *Tetrabiblos*). An Albertus Magnus, a St. Thomas, a Roger Bacon, a Dante (*Convivio*, II, Ch. 14), and many others believe that the cycles and periodicities of the world's history are governed by the influence of the stars, whether this influence obeys the will of God and is his instrument in history or whether—a hypothesis that gains increasing adherence—it is regarded as a force immanent in the cosmos.[5] In short, to adopt Sorokin's formulation, the Middle Ages are dominated by the eschatological conception (in its two essential moments: the creation and the end of the world), complemented by the theory of cyclic undulation that explains the periodic return of events. This twofold dogma dominates speculation down to the seventeenth century, although, at the same time, a theory of

[2] Pierre Duhem, *Le Système du monde* (Paris, 1913–17); Lynn Thorndike, *A History of Magic and Experimental Science* (New York, 1929–41); Pitirim A. Sorokin, *Social and Cultural Dynamics*, II (New York, 1937–41).

[3] Thorndike, I, pp. 455 ff.; Sorokin, p. 371.

[4] Duhem, V, pp. 223 ff.

[5] Ibid., pp. 225 ff.; Thorndike, II, pp. 267 ff., 416 ff., etc.; Sorokin, p. 371.

the linear progress of history begins to assert itself. In the Middle Ages, the germs of this theory can be recognized in the writings of Albertus Magnus and St. Thomas; but it is with the *Eternal Gospel* of Joachim of Floris that it appears in all its coherence, as an integral element of a magnificent eschatology of history, the most significant contribution of Christianity in this field since St. Augustine's. Joachim of Floris divides the history of the world into three great epochs, successively inspired and dominated by a different person of the Trinity: Father, Son, Holy Ghost. In the Calabrian abbot's vision, each of these epochs reveals, in history, a new dimension of the divinity and, by this fact, allows humanity to perfect itself progressively until finally, in the last phase—inspired by the Holy Ghost—it arrives at absolute spiritual freedom.[6]

But, as we said, the tendency which gains increasing adherence is that of an immanentization of the cyclical theory. Side by side with voluminous astrological treatises, the considerations of scientific astronomy assert themselves. So it is that in the theories of Tycho Brahe, Kepler, Cardano, Giordano Bruno, or Campanella, the cyclical ideology survives beside the new conception of linear progress professed, for example, by a Francis Bacon or a Pascal. From the seventeenth century on, linearism and the progressivistic conception of history assert themselves more and more, inaugurating faith in an infinite progress, a faith already proclaimed by Leibniz, predominant in the century of "enlightenment," and popularized in the nine-

[6] It was a real tragedy for the Western world that Joachim of Floris' prophetico-eschatological speculations, though they inspired and fertilized the thought of a St. Francis of Assisi, of a Dante, and of a Savonarola, so quickly sank into oblivion, the Calabrian monk surviving only as a name to which could be attached a multitude of apocryphal writings. The immanence of spiritual freedom, not only in respect to dogma but also in respect to society (a freedom that Joachim conceived as a necessity of both divine and historical dialectics), was again professed, at a later period, by the ideologies of the Reformation and the Renaissance, but in entirely different terms and in accordance with different spiritual views.

teenth century by the triumph of the ideas of the evolutionists. We must wait until our own century to see the beginnings of certain new reactions against this historical linearism and a certain revival of interest in the theory of cycles; [7] so it is that, in political economy, we are witnessing the rehabilitation of the notions of cycle, fluctuation, periodic oscillation; that in philosophy the myth of eternal return is revivified by Nietzsche; or that, in the philosophy of history, a Spengler or a Toynbee concern themselves with the problem of periodicity. [8]

In connection with this rehabilitation of cyclical conceptions, Sorokin rightly observes [9] that present theories concerning the death of the universe do not exclude the hypothesis of the creation of a new universe, somewhat after the fashion of the Great Year in Greco-Oriental speculation or of the yuga cycle in the thought of India (see above, pp. 113 ff.). Basically, it may be said that it is only in the cyclical theories of modern times that the meaning of the archaic myth of eternal repetition realizes its full implications. For the medieval cyclical theories confined themselves to justifying the periodicity of events by giving them an integral place in the rhythms of the cosmos and the fatalities of the stars. They thereby also implicitly affirmed the cyclical repetition of the events of history, even when this repetition was not regarded as continuing *ad infinitum*. Even more: by the fact that historical events depended upon cycles and astral situations, they became intelligible and even foreseeable, since they thus acquired a transcend-

---

[7] Sorokin, pp. 379 ff.

[8] Cf. A. Rey, *Le Retour éternel et la philosophie de la physique* (Paris, 1927); Pitirim A. Sorokin, *Contemporary Sociological Theories* (New York, 1928), pp. 728–41; Arnold J. Toynbee, *A Study of History*, III (London, 1934); Ellsworth Huntington, *Mainsprings of Civilization* (New York, 1945), especially pp. 453 ff.; Jean Claude Antoine, "L'Éternel Retour de l'histoire deviendra-t-il objet de science?," *Critique* (Paris), XXVII (Aug., 1948), 723 ff.

[9] Sorokin, p. 383, note 80.

ent *model*; the wars, famines, and wretchedness provoked
by contemporary history were at most only the repetition
of an archetype, itself determined by the stars and by
celestial norms from which the divine will was not always
absent. As at the close of antiquity, these new expressions
of the myth of eternal return were above all appreciated
among the intellectual elites and especially consoled those
who directly suffered the pressure of history. The peasant
masses, in antiquity as in modern times, took less interest
in cyclical and astral formulas; indeed, they found their
consolation and support in the concept of archetypes and
repetition, a concept that they "lived" less on the plane
of the cosmos and the stars than on the mythico-historical
level (transforming, for example, historical personages
into exemplary heroes, historical events into mythical categories, and so on, in accordance with the dialectic which
we defined above, pp. 37 ff.).

The Difficulties of Historicism

THE REAPPEARANCE of cyclical theories in contemporary
thought is pregnant with meaning. Incompetent as we are
to pass judgment upon their validity, we shall confine ourselves to observing that the formulation, in modern terms,
of an archaic myth betrays at least the desire to find a
meaning and a transhistorical justification for historical
events. Thus we find ourselves once again in the pre-
Hegelian position, the validity of the "historicistic" solutions, from Hegel to Marx, being implicitly called into
question. From Hegel on, every effort is directed toward
saving and conferring value on the historical event as such,
the event in itself and for itself. In his study of the German
Constitution, Hegel wrote that if we recognize that things

are necessarily as they are, that is, that they are not arbitrary and not the result of chance, we shall at the same time recognize that they *must* be as they are. A century later, the concept of historical necessity will enjoy a more and more triumphant practical application: in fact, all the cruelties, aberrations, and tragedies of history have been, and still are, justified by the necessities of the "historical moment." Probably Hegel did not intend to go so far. But since he had resolved to reconcile himself with his own historical moment, he was obliged to see in every event the will of the Universal Spirit. This is why he considered "reading the morning papers a sort of realistic benediction of the morning." For him, only daily contact with events could orient man's conduct in his relations with the world and with God.

How could Hegel know what was *necessary* in history, what, consequently, must occur exactly as it had occurred? Hegel believed that he knew what the Universal Spirit wanted. We shall not insist upon the audacity of this thesis, which, after all, abolishes precisely what Hegel wanted to save in history—human freedom. But there is an aspect of Hegel's philosophy of history that interests us because it still preserves something of the Judaeo-Christian conception: for Hegel, the historical event was the manifestation of the Universal Spirit. Now, it is possible to discern a parallel between Hegel's philosophy of history and the theology of history of the Hebrew prophets: for the latter, as for Hegel, an event is irreversible and valid in itself inasmuch as it is a new manifestation of the will of God—a proposition really revolutionary, we should remind ourselves, from the viewpoint of traditional societies dominated by the eternal repetition of archetypes. Thus, in Hegel's view, the destiny of a people still preserved a transhistorical significance, because all history revealed a new and more perfect manifestation of the Universal Spirit. But with Marx, history cast off all transcendental significance; it was no longer anything more than the epiphany of the class struggle. To what extent could such a theory justify historical sufferings? For the answer, we have but to turn to the pathetic resistance of a Belinsky or a Dostoevski, for example, who asked themselves how, from the viewpoint of the Hegelian and Marxian dialectic, it was possible to redeem all the dramas of oppression, the collective sufferings, deportations, humiliations, and massacres that fill universal history.

Yet Marxism preserves a meaning to history. For Marxism, events are not a succession of arbitrary accidents; they exhibit a coherent structure and, above all, they lead to a definite end—final elimination of the terror of history, "salvation." Thus, at the end of the Marxist philosophy of history, lies the age of gold of the archaic eschatologies. In this sense it is correct to say not only that Marx "brought Hegel's philosophy back to earth" but also that he reconfirmed, upon an exclusively human level, the value of the primitive myth of the age of gold, with the difference that he puts the age of gold only at the end of history, instead of putting it at the beginning too. Here, for the militant Marxist, lies the secret of the remedy for the terror of history: just as the contemporaries of a "dark age" consoled themselves for their increasing sufferings by the thought that the aggravation of evil hastens final deliverance, so the militant Marxist of our day reads, in the drama provoked by the pressure of history, a necessary evil, the premonitory symptom of the approaching victory that will put an end forever to all historical "evil."

The terror of history becomes more and more intolerable from the viewpoints afforded by the various historicistic philosophies. For in them, of course, every historical event finds its full and only meaning in its reali-zation alone. We need not here enter into the theoretical difficulties of historicism, which already troubled Rickert, Troeltsch, Dilthey, and Simmel, and which the recent ef-forts of Croce, of Karl Mannheim, or of Ortega y Gasset have but partially overcome.[10] This essay does not require us to discuss either the philosophical value of historicism as such or the possibility of establishing a "philosophy of history" that should definitely transcend relativism. Dilthey himself, at the age of seventy, recognized that "the relativity of all human concepts is the last word of the historical vision of the world." In vain did he proclaim an *allgemeine Lebenserfahrung* as the final means of transcend-ing this relativity. In vain did Meinecke invoke "examina-tion of conscience" as a transsubjective experience capable of transcending the relativity of historical life. Heidegger had gone to the trouble of showing that the historicity of human existence forbids all hope of transcending time and history.

For our purpose, only one question concerns us: How can the "terror of history" be tolerated from the view-point of historicism? Justification of a historical event by the simple fact that it is a historical event, in other words, by the simple fact that it "happened that way," will not go far toward freeing humanity from the terror that the event inspires. Be it understood that we are not here con-cerned with the problem of evil, which, from whatever

[10] Let us say, first of all, that the terms "historism" or "historicism" cover many different and antagonistic philosophical currents and orientations. It is enough to recall Dilthey's vitalistic relativism, Croce's *storicismo*, Gentile's *attualismo*, and Ortega's "historical reason" to realize the multiplicity of philosophical valuations accorded to history during the first half of the twentieth century. For Croce's present position, see his *La storia come pensiero e come azione* (Bari, 1938; 7th rev. edn., 1965). Also J. Ortega y Gasset, *Historia como sistema* (Madrid, 1941); Karl Mannheim, *Ideology and Utopia* (trans. by Louis Wirth and Edward Shils, New York, 1936). On the problem of history, see also Pedro Lain Entralgo, *Medicina e historia* (Madrid, 1941); and Karl Löwith, *Meaning in History* (Chicago, 1949).

angle it be viewed, remains a philosophical and religious problem; we are concerned with the problem of history as history, of the "evil" that is bound up not with man's condition but with his behavior toward others. We should wish to know, for example, how it would be possible to tolerate, and to justify, the sufferings and annihilation of so many peoples who suffer and are annihilated for the simple reason that their geographical situation sets them in the pathway of history; that they are neighbors of empires in a state of permanent expansion. How justify, for example, the fact that southeastern Europe had to suffer for centuries—and hence to renounce any impulse toward a higher historical existence, toward spiritual creation on the universal plane—for the sole reason that it happened to be on the road of the Asiatic invaders and later the neighbor of the Ottoman Empire? And in our day, when historical pressure no longer allows any escape, how can man tolerate the catastrophes and horrors of history—from collective deportations and massacres to atomic bombings —if beyond them he can glimpse no sign, no transhistorical meaning; if they are only the blind play of economic, social, or political forces, or, even worse, only the result of the "liberties" that a minority takes and exercises directly on the stage of universal history?

We know how, in the past, humanity has been able to endure the sufferings we have enumerated: they were regarded as a punishment inflicted by God, the syndrome of the decline of the "age," and so on. And it was possible to accept them precisely because they had a metahistorical meaning, because, for the greater part of mankind, still clinging to the traditional viewpoint, history did not have, and could not have, value in itself. Every hero repeated the archetypal gesture, every war rehearsed the struggle between good and evil, every fresh social injustice was identified with the sufferings of the Saviour (or, for example, in the pre-Christian world, with the passion of a divine messenger or vegetation god), each new massacre repeated the glorious end of the martyrs. It is not our part to decide whether such motives were puerile or not, or whether such a refusal of history always proved efficacious. In our opinion, only one fact counts: by virtue of this view, tens of millions of men were able, for century after century, to endure great historical pressures without despairing, without committing suicide or falling into that spiritual aridity that always brings with it a relativistic or nihilistic view of history.

Moreover, as we have already observed, a very considerable fraction of the population of Europe, to say nothing of the other continents, still lives today by the light of the traditional, anti-"historicistic" viewpoint. Hence it is above all the "elites" that are confronted with the problem, since they alone are forced, and with increasing rigor, to take cognizance of their historical situation. It is true that Christianity and the eschatological philosophy of history have not ceased to satisfy a considerable proportion of these elites. Up to a certain point, and for certain individuals, it may be said that Marxism—especially in its popular forms—represents a defense against the terror of history. Only the historicistic position, in all its varieties and shades—from Nietzsche's "destiny" to Heidegger's "temporality"—remains disarmed.[11] It is by no means mere fortuitious coincidence that, in this philoso-

---

[11] We take the liberty of emphasizing that "historicism" was created and professed above all by thinkers belonging to nations for which history has never been a continuous terror. These thinkers would perhaps have adopted another viewpoint had they belonged to nations marked by the "fatality of history." It would certainly be interesting, in any case, to know if the theory according to which everything that happens is "good," simply *because* it has happened, would have been accepted without qualms by the thinkers of the Baltic countries, of the Balkans, or of colonial territories.

phy, despair, the *amor fati*, and pessimism are elevated to the rank of heroic virtues and instruments of cognition.

Yet this position, although the most modern and, in a certain sense, almost the inevitable position for all thinkers who define man as a "historical being," has not yet made a definitive conquest of contemporary thought. Some pages earlier, we noted various recent orientations that tend to reconfer value upon the myth of cyclical periodicity, even the myth of eternal return. These orientations disregard not only historicism but even history as such. We believe we are justified in seeing in them, rather than a resistance to history, a revolt against historical *time*, an attempt to restore this historical time, freighted as it is with human experience, to a place in the time that is cosmic, cyclical, and infinite. In any case it is worth noting that the work of two of the most significant writers of our day—T. S. Eliot and James Joyce—is saturated with nostalgia for the myth of eternal repetition and, in the last analysis, for the abolition of time. There is also reason to foresee that, as the terror of history grows worse, as existence becomes more and more precarious because of history, the positions of historicism will increasingly lose in prestige. And, at a moment when history could do what neither the cosmos, nor man, nor chance have yet succeeded in doing—that is, wipe out the human race in its entirety—it may be that we are witnessing a desperate attempt to prohibit the "events of history" through a reintegration of human societies within the horizon (artificial, because decreed) of archetypes and their repetition. In other words, it is not inadmissible to think of an epoch, and an epoch not too far distant, when humanity, to ensure its survival, will find itself reduced to desisting from any further "making" of history in the sense in which it began to make it from the creation of the first empires, will confine itself to repeating prescribed archetypal gestures, and will strive to forget, as meaningless and dangerous, any spontaneous gesture which might entail "historical" consequences. It would even be interesting to compare the anhistorical solution of future societies with the paradisal or eschatological myths of the golden age of the beginning or the end of the world. But as we have it in mind to pursue these speculations elsewhere, let us now return to our problem: the position of historical man in relation to archaic man, and let us attempt to understand the objections brought against the latter on the basis of the historicistic view.

Freedom and History

IN HIS rejection of concepts of periodicity and hence, in the last analysis, of the archaic concepts of archetypes and repetition, we are, we believe, justified in seeing modern man's resistance to nature, the will of "historical man" to affirm his autonomy. As Hegel remarked, with noble self-assurance, nothing new ever occurs in nature. And the crucial difference between the man of the archaic civilizations and modern, historical man lies in the increasing value the latter gives to historical events, that is, to the "novelties" that, for traditional man, represented either meaningless conjunctures or infractions of norms (hence "faults," "sins," and so on) and that, as such, required to be expelled (abolished) periodically. The man who adopts the historical viewpoint would be justified in regarding the traditional conception of archetypes and repetition as an aberrant reidentification of history (that is, of "freedom" and "novelty") with nature (in which everything repeats itself). For, as modern man can observe, archetypes themselves constitute a "history" insofar as they are made up of gestures, acts, and decrees that, although supposed to have been manifested *in illo tempore*, were nevertheless manifested, that is, came to birth in time, "took place," like any other historical event. Primitive myths often mention the birth, activity, and disappearance of a god or a hero whose "civilizing" gestures are thenceforth repeated *ad infinitum*. This comes down to saying that archaic man also knows a history, although it is a primordial history, placed in a mythical time. Archaic man's rejection of history, his refusal to situate himself in a concrete, historical time, would, then, be the symptom of a precocious weariness, a fear of movement and spontaneity; in short, placed between accepting the historical condition and its risks on the one hand, and his reidentification with the modes of nature on the other, he would choose such a reidentification.

In this total adherence, on the part of archaic man, to archetypes and repetition, modern man would be justified in seeing not only the primitives' amazement at their own first spontaneous and creative free gestures and their veneration, repeated *ad infinitum*, but also a feeling of guilt on the part of man hardly emerged from the paradise of animality (i.e., from nature), a feeling that urges him to reidentify with nature's eternal repetition the few primordial, creative, and spontaneous gestures that had signalized the appearance of freedom. Continuing his critique, modern man could even read in this fear, this hesitation or fatigue in the presence of any gesture without an archetype, nature's tendency toward equilibrium and rest; and he would read this tendency in the anticlimax that fatally follows upon any exuberant gesture of life and that some have gone so far as to recognize in the need felt by human reason to unify the real through knowledge. In the last analysis, modern man, who accepts history or claims to accept it, can reproach archaic man, imprisoned within the mythical horizon of archetypes and repetition, with his creative impotence, or, what amounts to the same thing, his inability to accept the risks entailed by every creative act. For the modern man can be creative only insofar as he is historical; in other words, all creation is forbidden him except that which has its source in his own freedom; and, consequently, everything is denied him except the freedom to make history by making himself.

To these criticisms raised by modern man, the man of the traditional civilizations could reply by a countercriticism that would at the same time be a defense of the type of archaic existence. It is becoming more and more doubtful, he might say, if modern man can make history. On the contrary, the more modern [12] he becomes—that is, without defenses against the terror of history—the less chance he has of himself making history. For history either makes itself (as the result of the seed sown by acts that occurred in the past, several centuries or even several millennia ago; we will cite the consequences of the discovery of agriculture or metallurgy, of the Industrial Revolution in the eighteenth century, and so on) or it tends to be made by an increasingly smaller number of men who not only prohibit the mass of their contemporaries from directly or indirectly intervening in the history they are making (or which the small group is making), but in addition have at their disposal means sufficient to force each individual to endure, for his own part, the consequences of this history, that is, to live immediately and continuously in dread of history. Modern man's boasted freedom to make history is illusory for nearly the whole of the human race. At most,

[12] It is well to make clear that, in this context, "modern man" is such in his insistence upon being exclusively historical; i.e., that he is, above all, the "man" of historicism, of Marxism, and of existentialism. It is superfluous to add that not all of our contemporaries recognize themselves in such a man.

man is left free to choose between two positions: (1) to oppose the history that is being made by the very small minority (and, in this case, he is free to choose between suicide and deportation); (2) to take refuge in a subhuman existence or in flight. The "freedom" that historical existence implies was possible—and even then within certain limits—at the beginning of the modern period, but it tends to become inaccessible as the period becomes more historical, by which we mean more alien from any transhistorical model. It is perfectly natural, for example, that Marxism and Fascism must lead to the establishment of two types of historical existence: that of the leader (the only really "free" man) and that of the followers, who find, in the historical existence of the leader, not an archetype of their own existence but the lawgiver of the gestures that are provisionally permitted them.

Thus, for traditional man, modern man affords the type neither of a free being nor of a creator of history. On the contrary, the man of the archaic civilizations can be proud of his mode of existence, which allows him to be free and to create. He is free to be no longer what he was, free to annul his own history through periodic abolition of time and collective regeneration. This freedom in respect to his own history—which, for the modern, is not only irreversible but constitutes human existence—cannot be claimed by the man who wills to be historical. We know that the archaic and traditional societies granted freedom each year to begin a new, a "pure" existence, with virgin possibilities. And there is no question of seeing in this an imitation of nature, which also undergoes periodic regeneration, "beginning anew" each spring, with each spring recovering all its powers intact. Indeed, whereas nature repeats itself, each new spring being the same eternal spring (that is, the repetition of the Creation), archaic man's "purity" after the periodic abolition of time and the recovery of his virtualities intact allows him, on the threshold of each "new life," a continued existence in eternity and hence the definitive abolition, *hic et nunc*, of profane time. The intact "possibilities" of nature each spring and archaic man's possibilities on the threshold of each year are, then, not homologous. Nature recovers only itself, whereas archaic man recovers the possibility of definitively transcending time and living in eternity. Insofar as he fails to do so, insofar as he "sins," that is, falls into historical existence, into time, he each year thwarts the possibility. At least he retains the freedom to annul his faults, to wipe out the memory of his "fall into history," and to make another attempt to escape definitively from time.[13]

Furthermore, archaic man certainly has the right to consider himself more creative than modern man, who sees himself as creative only in respect to history. Every year, that is, archaic man takes part in the repetition of the cosmogony, the creative act *par excellence*. We may even add that, for a certain time, man was creative on the cosmic plane, imitating this periodic cosmogony (which he also repeated on all the other planes of life, cf. pp. 80 ff.) and participating in it.[14] We should also bear in mind the "creationistic" implications of the Oriental philosophies and techniques (especially the Indian), which thus find a place in the same traditional horizon. The East unanimously rejects the idea of the ontological irreducibility of the existent, even though it too sets out from a sort of "existentialism" (i.e., from acknowledging suffering as the situation of any possible cosmic condition). Only, the East does not accept the destiny of the human being as final and irreducible. Oriental techniques attempt above all to

[13] On this, see our *Patterns in Comparative Religion* (English trans., London and New York, 1958), pp. 398 ff.

[14] Not to mention the possibilities of "magical creation," which exist in traditional societies, and which are real.

annul or transcend the human condition. In this respect, it is justifiable to speak not only of freedom (in the positive sense) or deliverance (in the negative sense) but actually of creation; for what is involved is creating a new man and creating him on a suprahuman plane, a man-god, such as the imagination of historical man has never dreamed it possible to create.

Despair or Faith

HOWEVER this may be, our dialogue between archaic man and modern man does not affect our problem. Whatever be the truth in respect to the freedom and the creative virtualities of historical man, it is certain that none of the historicistic philosophies is able to defend him from the terror of history. We could even imagine a final attempt: to save history and establish an ontology of history, events would be regarded as a series of "situations" by virtue of which the human spirit should attain knowledge of levels of reality otherwise inaccessible to it. This attempt to justify history is not without interest,[15] and we anticipate returning to the subject elsewhere. But we are able to observe here and now that such a position affords a shelter from the terror of history only insofar as it postulates the existence at least of the Universal Spirit. What consolation

[15] It is only through some such reasoning that it would be possible to found a sociology of knowledge that should not lead to relativism and skepticism. The "influences"—economic, social, national, cultural—that affect "ideologies" (in the sense which Karl Mannheim gave the term) would not annul their objective value any more than the fever or the intoxication that reveals to a poet a new poetic creation impairs the value of the latter. All these social, economic, and other influences would, on the contrary, be occasions for envisaging a spiritual universe from new angles. But it goes without saying that a sociology of knowledge, that is, the study of the social conditioning of ideologies, could avoid relativism only by affirming the autonomy of the spirit—which, if we understand him aright, Karl Mannheim did not dare to affirm.

should we find in knowing that the sufferings of millions of men have made possible the revelation of a limitary situation of the human condition if, beyond that limitary situation, there should be only nothingness? Again, there is no question here of judging the validity of a historicistic philosophy, but only of establishing to what extent such a philosophy can exorcise the terror of history. If, for historical tragedies to be excused, it suffices that they should be regarded as the means by which man has been enabled to know the limit of human resistance, such an excuse can in no way make man less haunted by the terror of history.

Basically, the horizon of archetypes and repetition cannot be transcended with impunity unless we accept a philosophy of freedom that does not exclude God. And indeed this proved to be true when the horizon of archetypes and repetition was transcended, for the first time, by Judaeo-Christianism, which introduced a new category into religious experience: the category of *faith*. It must not be forgotten that, if Abraham's faith can be defined as "for God everything is possible," the faith of Christianity implies that everything is also possible for man. ". . . Have faith in God. For verily I say unto you, That whosoever shall say unto this mountain, Be thou removed, and be thou cast into the sea; and shall not doubt in his heart, but shall believe that those things which he saith shall come to pass; he shall have whatsoever he saith. Therefore I say unto you, What things soever ye desire, when ye pray, believe that ye receive them, and ye shall have them" (Mark 11 : 22–24).[16] Faith, in this context, as in many others, means absolute emancipation from any kind of natural "law" and hence the highest freedom that man can imagine: freedom to intervene even in the ontological con-

[16] Such affirmations must not be complacently dismissed merely because they imply the possibility of miracle. If miracles have been so rare since the appearance of Christianity, the blame rests not on Christianity but on Christians.

stitution of the universe. It is, consequently, a pre-eminently creative freedom. In other words, it constitutes a new formula for man's collaboration with the creation—the first, but also the only such formula accorded to him since the traditional horizon of archetypes and repetition was transcended. Only such a freedom (aside from its soteriological, hence, in the strict sense, its religious value) is able to defend modern man from the terror of history—a freedom, that is, which has its source and finds its guaranty and support in God. Every other modern freedom, whatever satisfactions it may procure to him who possesses it, is powerless to justify history; and this, for every man who is sincere with himself, is equivalent to the terror of history.

We may say, furthermore, that Christianity is the "religion" of modern man and historical man, of the man who simultaneously discovered personal freedom and continuous time (in place of cyclical time). It is even interesting to note that the existence of God forced itself far more urgently upon modern man, for whom history exists as such, as history and not as repetition, than upon the man of the archaic and traditional cultures, who, to defend himself from the terror of history, had at his disposition all the myths, rites, and customs mentioned in the course of this book. Moreover, although the idea of God and the religious experiences that it implies existed from the most distant ages, they could be, and were, replaced at times by other religious "forms" (totemism, cult of ancestors, Great Goddesses of fecundity, and so on) that more promptly answered the religious needs of primitive humanity. In the horizon of archetypes and repetition, the terror of history, when it appeared, could be supported. Since the "invention" of faith, in the Judaeo-Christian sense of the word (= for God all is possible), the man who has left the horizon of archetypes and repetition can no longer defend himself against that terror except through the idea of God. In fact, it is only by presupposing the existence of God that he conquers, on the one hand, freedom (which grants him autonomy in a universe governed by laws or, in other words, the "inauguration" of a mode of being that is new and unique in the universe) and, on the other hand, the certainty that historical tragedies have a transhistorical meaning, even if that meaning is not always visible for humanity in its present condition. Any other situation of modern man leads, in the end, to despair. It is a despair provoked not by his own human existentiality, but by his presence in a historical universe in which almost the whole of mankind lives prey to a continual terror (even if not always conscious of it).

In this respect, Christianity incontestibly proves to be the religion of "fallen man": and this to the extent to which modern man is irremediably identified with history and progress, and to which history and progress are a fall, both implying the final abandonment of the paradise of archetypes and repetition.

BIBLIOGRAPHY

NOTE: For references to the *Śatapatha Brāhmaṇa, Upaniṣads,* etc., see *The Sacred Books of the East* (F. Max Müller, ed., Oxford, 1879–1910). For the Bible, see the King James Version. For the Apocrypha and Pseudepigrapha, see *The Apocrypha and Pseudepigrapha of the Old Testament in English* (R. H. Charles, ed., Oxford, 1913). For items preceded by an asterisk, see the Addenda, p. 173.

ABEGG, EMIL. *Der Messiasglaube in Indien und Iran.* Berlin, 1928.

AL-BĪRŪNĪ. *See* BĪRŪNĪ, MUHAMMAD IBN AHMAD AL-.

ALBRIGHT, WILLIAM FOXWELL. "The Mouth of the Rivers," *The American Journal of Semitic Languages and Literatures* (Chicago), XXXV (1919), 161–95.

ANTOINE, JEAN CLAUDE. "L'Éternel Retour de l'histoire deviendra-t-il objet de science?" *Critique* (Paris), XXVII (Aug., 1948), 723 ff.

ARNIM, H. F. A. VON. *Stoicorum veterum fragmenta.* Leipzig, 1903–24. 4 vols.

AUTRAN, CHARLES. *L'Epopée indoue.* Paris, 1946.

BIDEZ, JOSEPH. *Éos, ou Platon et l'Orient.* Brussels, 1945.

BIGNONE, ETTORE. *Empedocle.* Turin, 1916.

BĪRŪNĪ, MUHAMMAD IBN AHMAD AL-. *The Chronology of Ancient Nations.* Trans. C. Edward Sachau. London, 1879.

BLEICHSTEINER, ROBERT. *L'Église jaune.* [French trans.] Paris, 1937.

BOUSSET, WILHELM. *Der Antichrist in der Überlieferung des Judentums, des Neuen Testaments und der alten Kirche.* Göttingen, 1895.

BRIEM, EFRAIM. *Les Sociétés secrètes des mystères.* Trans. from the Swedish by E. Guerre. Paris, 1941.

BUDGE, SIR E. A. WALLIS (tr.). *The Book of the Cave of Treasures.* Trans. from the Syriac. London, 1927.

BURROWS, E. "Some Cosmological Patterns in Babylonian Religion," *The Labyrinth,* ed. S. H. Hooke (London, 1935), pp. 45–70.

CALLAWAY, HENRY. *The Religious System of the Amazulu.* London, 1869.

CARAMAN, PETRU. "Geneza baladei istorice," *Anuarul Arhivei de Folklor* (Bucharest), I–II (1933–34).

CARCOPINO, JÉRÔME. *Virgile et le mystère de la IVe églogue.* Rev. and enl. edn., Paris, 1943.

CHADWICK, H. MUNRO and N. K. *The Growth of Literature.* Cambridge, 1932–40. 3 vols.

CHARLES, ROBERT HENRY (ed.). *The Apocrypha and Pseudepigrapha of the Old Testament in English.* Oxford, 1913. 2 vols.

CHASE, DRUMMOND PERCY. *The Ethics of Aristotle.* London, 1934.

CHIERA, EDWARD. *Sumerian Religious Texts.* Upland, 1924.

CHRISTENSEN, ARTHUR. *Les Types du premier homme et du premier roi dans l'histoire légendaire des Iraniens.* Stockholm, 1917. 2 vols.

COOMARASWAMY, ANANDA K. *The Ṛg Veda as Land-náma-bók.* London, 1935.

———. *The Darker Side of Dawn.* Washington, 1935.

———. "Vedic Exemplarism," *Harvard Journal of Asiatic Studies*, I (1936), 44–64.

———. "The Philosophy of Mediaeval and Oriental Art," *Zalmoxis* (Paris and Bucharest), I (1938), 20–49.

———. "Sir Gawain and the Green Knight: Indra and Namuci," *Speculum* (Cambridge, Mass.), Jan., 1944, pp. 1–23.

———. *Figures of Speech or Figures of Thought.* London, 1946.

*CORBIN, HENRY. "Le Temps cyclique dans le mazdéisme et dans l'ismaélisme." *Eranos-Jahrbuch*, XX (Zurich, 1951), pp. 149–217.

CROCE, BENEDETTO. *La storia come pensiero e come azione*, Bari, 1938; 7th rev. edn., Bari, 1965.

CUMONT, FRANZ. "La Fin du monde selon les mages occidentaux," *Revue de l'Histoire des Religions* (Paris), Jan.–June, 1931.

DAEHNHARDT, OSKAR. *Natursagen.* Leipzig, 1907–12. 4 vols.

DARMESTETER, JAMES (trans.). *Le Zend-Avesta.* Paris, 1892–93. 3 vols.

DELATTE, ARMAND. *Herbarius.* 2nd edn., Liége, 1938.

DOMBART, THEODOR. *Der Sakralturm.* Pt. I: *Zikkurrat.* Munich, 1920.

DROWER, E. S. (E. S. Stevens). *The Mandaeans of Iraq and Iran.* Oxford, 1937.

BIBLIOGRAPHY

DUHEM, PIERRE. *Le Système du monde.* Paris, 1913–17. 5 vols.

DUMÉZIL, GEORGES. *Le Problème des centaures.* Paris, 1929.

―――. *Ouranós-Váruṇa.* Paris, 1934.

―――. *Mythes et dieux des Germains.* Paris, 1939.

―――. *Horace et les Curiaces.* Paris, 1942.

EDSMAN, C. M. *Le Baptême de feu.* Uppsala, 1940.

ELIADE, MIRCEA. *Yoga. Essai sur les origines de la mystique indienne.* Paris and Bucharest, 1936.

―――. *Cosmologie şi alchimie babiloniană.* Bucharest, 1937.

―――. *Comentarii la legenda Meşterului Manole.* Bucharest, 1943.

―――. "La Mandragore et le mythe de la 'naissance miraculeuse,' " *Zalmoxis* (Paris and Bucharest), III (1943), 1–52.

―――. *Techniques du Yoga.* Paris, 1948.

*―――. *Traité d'histoire des religions.* Paris, 1949.

*―――. "Le Temps et l'éternité dans la pensée indienne," *Eranos-Jahrbuch,* XX (Zurich, 1951), pp. 219–52.

*―――. *Le Chamanisme et les techniques archaïques de l'extase.* Paris, 1951.

*―――. *Images et symboles.* Paris, 1952.

ENGNELL, IVAN. *Studies in Divine Kingship in the Ancient Near East.* Uppsala, 1943.

FOY, WILLY. "Indische Kultbauten als Symbole des Götterbergs," *Festschrift Ernst Windisch zum siebzigsten Geburtstag . . . dargebracht* (Leipzig, 1914), pp. 213–16.

FRANKFORT, HENRI. "Gods and Myths in Sargonid Seals," *Iraq* (London), I (1934), 2–29.

FRAZER, SIR JAMES GEORGE. *Folklore in the Old Testament.* London, 1918. 3 vols.

―――. *The Golden Bough.* 3rd edn., London, 1907–15. 12 vols. Especially Part IV: *Adonis, Attis, Osiris,* and Part VI: *The Scapegoat.*

FURLANI, GIUSEPPE. *Religione dei Yezidi.* Bologna, 1930.

―――. *La religione degli Hittiti.* Bologna, 1936.

GAERTE, W. "Kosmische Vorstellungen im Bilde prähistorischer Zeit: Erdberg, Himmelsberg, Erdnabel und Weltströme," *Anthropos* (Salzburg), IX (1914), 956–79.

GASTER, THEODOR HERZL. *Thespis; Ritual, Myth and Drama in the Ancient Near East.* New York, 1950.

GENNEP, ARNOLD VAN. *Tabou et totémisme à Madagascar*. Paris, 1904.

GODDARD, PLINY EARLE. *Life and Culture of the Hupa*. (University of California Publications in American Archaeology and Ethnology, I, no. 1, pp. 1–88.) Berkeley, 1903.

GÖTZE, ALBRECHT. *Kleinasien*. Leipzig, 1933.

GRANET, MARCEL. *Danses et légendes de la Chine ancienne*. Paris, 1926. 2 vols.

————. *La Pensée chinoise*. Paris, 1934.

HANDY, EDWARD SMITH CRAIGHILL. *Polynesian Religion*. Honolulu, 1927.

HARVA, UNO (formerly Uno Holmberg). *Der Baum des Lebens*. (Annales Accademiae Scientiarum Fennicae.) Helsinki, 1923.

HASLUCK, F. W. *Christianity and Islam under the Sultans*. Oxford, 1929. 2 vols.

HASTEEN, KLAH. *Navajo Creation Myth; the Story of the Emergence*. (Mary C. Wheelwright, rec., Navajo Religion Series, I, Museum of Navajo Ceremonial Art.) Santa Fe, 1942.

HASTINGS, JAMES (ed.). *Encyclopaedia of Religion and Ethics*. New York, 1951. 12 vols.

HERTEL, JOHANNES. *Das indogermanische Neujahrsopfer im Veda*. Leipzig, 1938.

HOCART, ARTHUR MAURICE. *Kingship*. London, 1927.

————. *Le Progrès de l'homme*. [French trans.] Paris, 1935.

————. *Kings and Councillors*. Cairo, 1936.

HÖFLER, OTTO. *Kultische Geheimbünde der Germanen*. Frankfort on the Main, 1934.

HOLMBERG, UNO. *See* HARVA, UNO.

HOOKE, S. H. (ed.). *The Labyrinth*. London, 1935.

————. (ed.). *Myth and Ritual*. London, 1935.

————. *The Origins of Early Semitic Ritual*. London, 1938.

HOWITT, A. W. *The Native Tribes of South-East Australia*. London, 1904.

HUBAUX, JEAN. *Les Grands Mythes de Rome*. Paris, 1945.

HUME, R. E. *The Thirteen Principal Upanishads*. Oxford, 1931.

HUNTINGTON, ELLSWORTH. *Mainsprings of Civilization*. New York, 1945.

HUTH, OTTO. *Janus*. Bonn, 1932.

JEAN, CHARLES FRANÇOIS. *La Religion sumérienne.* Paris, 1931.

JEREMIAS, ALFRED. *Handbuch der altorientalischen Geisteskultur.* 2nd edn., Berlin and Leipzig, 1929.

JOHNSON, A. R. "The Rôle of the King in the Jerusalem Cultus," *The Labyrinth,* ed. S. H. Hooke (London, 1935), pp. 73–111.

KIRFEL, WILLIBALD. *Die Kosmographie der Inder.* Bonn, 1920.

KOPPERS, WILHELM. *Die Bhil in Zentralindien.* Horn, 1948.

KRICKEBERG, WALTER. "Bauform und Weltbild im alten Mexico," *Paideuma* (Bamberg), IV (1950), 295–333.

KROEBER, A. L. *Handbook of the Indians of California.* Washington, 1925.

——— and GIFFORD, E. W. *World Renewal, a Cult System of Native Northwest California.* (Anthropological Records, XIII, no. 1, University of California.) Berkeley, 1949.

LABAT, RENÉ. *Le Caractère religieux de la royauté assyro-babylonienne.* Paris, 1939.

LAIN ENTRALGO, PEDRO. *Medicina y historia.* Madrid, 1941.

LAMOTTE, ÉTIENNE. *Le Traité de la Grande Vertu de Sagesse de Nāgārjuna.* (Bibliothèque du Muséon, XVIII, University of Louvain.) Louvain, 1944.

LASSY, H. *Muharram Mysteries.* Helsinki, 1916.

LA VALLÉE-POUSSIN, LOUIS DE (trans.). *L'Abhidharmakośa.* Paris, 1923–26.

——— (trans.). *Vijñaptimātratāsiddhi.* Paris, 1929.

———. "Documents d'Abhidharma: la controverse du temps," *Mélanges chinois et bouddhiques* (Brussels), V (1937), 1–158.

LEEUW, GERARDUS VAN DER. *Phänomenologie der Religion.* Tübingen, 1933.

———. *L'Homme primitif et la religion.* [French trans.] Paris, 1940.

*——. "Urzeit und Endzeit," *Eranos-Jahrbuch,* XVII (Zurich, 1950), pp. 11–51.

LEHMANN, F. R. "Weltuntergang und Welterneuerung im Glauben schriftloser Völker," *Zeitschrift für Ethnologie* (Berlin), LXXI (1939).

——— and PEDERSEN. "Der Beweis für die Auferstehung im Koran," *Der Islam* (Strassburg), V, pp. 54–61.

LÉVY-BRUHL, LUCIEN. *La Mythologie primitive*. Paris, 1935.

LIUNGMAN, WALDEMAR. *Traditionswanderungen, Euphrat-Rhein*. Helsinki, 1937–38. 2 vols.

LODS, A. *Comptes rendus de l'Académie des Inscriptions*. Paris, 1943.

LÖWITH, KARL. *Meaning in History*. Chicago, 1949.

MACLEOD, WILLIAM CHRISTIE. *The Origin and History of Politics*. New York, 1931.

MALALAS, JOANNES. *Chronographia*. (Corpus scriptorum historiae byzantinae, XV.) Bonn, 1831.

MANKAD, D. R. "Manvantara-Caturyuga Method," *Annals of the Bhandarkar Oriental Research Institute* (Poona), XXIII, Silver Jubilee Volume (1942), 271–90.

MANNHARDT, J. W. E. *Wald- und Feldkulte*. 2nd edn., Berlin, 1904–1905. 2 vols.

MANNHEIM, KARL. *Ideology and Utopia*. Trans. by Louis Wirth and Edward Shils. New York, 1936. (A trans. of *Ideologie und Utopie*, Bonn, 1930, and "Wissenssoziologie," *Handwoerterbuch der Soziologie*, ed. Alfred Vierkandt, Stuttgart, 1931.)

MARQUART, JOSEF. "The Nawrôz, Its History and Its Significance," *Journal of the Cama Oriental Institute* (Bombay), XXXI (1937), 1–51.

MAUSS, MARCEL. "Essai sur le don, forme archaïque de l'échange," *Année Sociologique* (Paris), 2nd series, I (1923–24).

MAX MÜLLER, F. (ed.). *The Sacred Books of the East*. Oxford, 1879–1910. 50 vols.

MURKO, MATTHIAS. *La Poésie populaire épique en Yougoslavie au début du XXᵉ siècle*. Paris, 1929.

MUS, PAUL. *Barabudur*. (2nd vol. incomplete.) Hanoi, 1935 ff. 2 vols.

NILSSON, MARTIN P. *Primitive Time Reckoning*. (Acta Societatis Humaniorum Litterarum Lundensis, I.) Lund, 1920.

NOURRY, ÉMILE (P. Saintyves, pseud.). *Essais de folklore biblique*. Paris, 1923.

———. *L'Astrologie populaire*. Paris, 1937.

NYBERG, H. S. "Questions de cosmogonie et de cosmologie mazdéennes," *Journal Asiatique* (Paris), CCXIV (Apr.–June, 1929), pp. 193–310; CCXIX (July–Sept., 1931), pp. 1–134.

NYBERG, H. S. "Questions de cosmogonie et de cosmologie mazdéennes," *Journal Asiatique* (Paris), 1929, 1931.

———. Criticisms in *Monde Oriental* (Uppsala), XXIII (1929), 204–11.

OHRT, FERDINAND. "Herba, gratiâ plena," *FF Communications* (Helsinki), No. 82 (1929).

OKA, MASAO. "Kulturschichten in Altjapan." Unpublished German trans. of the Japanese MS.

ORTEGA Y GASSET, JOSÉ. *Historia como sistema.* Madrid, 1941.

PALLIS, SVEND AAGE. *The Babylonian Akîtu Festival.* Copenhagen, 1926.

PARROT, A. *Ziggurats et Tour de Babel.* Paris, 1949.

PATAI, RAPHAEL. *Man and Temple.* London, 1947.

PETTAZZONI, RAFFAELE. *La confessione dei peccati.* Bologna, 1929–36. 3 vols.

———. "Der babylonische Ritus des Akîtu and das Gedicht der Weltschöpfung," *Eranos-Jahrbuch*, XIX (Zurich, 1950), pp. 403–30.

———. "Io and Rangi," *Pro regno pro sanctuario, hommage à G. van der Leeuw* (Nijkerk, 1950), pp. 359–64.

PINCHERLE, ALBERTO. *Gli Oracoli Sibillini giudaici.* Rome, 1922.

POLAK, JAKOB EDUARD. *Persien. Das Land und seine Bewohner.* Leipzig, 1865. 2 vols.

*PUECH, HENRI-CHARLES. "La Gnose et le temps," *Eranos-Jahrbuch*, XX (Zurich, 1951), pp. 57–113.

———. "Temps, histoire et mythe dans le christianisme des premiers siècles," *Proceedings of the VIIth Congress for the History of Religion* (Amsterdam, 1951), pp. 33–52.

REY, A. *Le Retour éternel et la philosophie de la physique.* Paris, 1927.

ROCK, F. "Das Jahr von 360 Tagen und seine Gliederung," *Wiener Beiträge zur Kulturgeschichte und Linguistik*, I (1930), 253–88.

ROEDER, GÜNTHER (ed.). *Urkunden zur Religion des alten Ägypten.* Jena, 1915.

ROSCHER, WILHELM HEINRICH. "Neue Omphalosstudien," *Abhandlungen der Königlich Sächsischen Gesellschaft der Wissenschaft* (Leipzig), *Phil.-hist. Klasse*, XXXI, 1 (1915).

Sacred Books of the East, The. See MAX MÜLLER, F.

SAINTYVES, P. See NOURRY, ÉMILE.

SCHAEDER, HANS HEINRICH. "Der iranische Zeitgott und sein Mythos," *Zeitschrift der Deutschen Morgenländischen Gesellschaft* (Leipzig), XCV (1941), 268 ff.

SCHAYER, STANISLAW. *Contributions to the Problem of Time in Indian Philosophy.* Cracow, 1938.

SCHEBESTA, PAUL. *Les Pygmées.* [French trans.] Paris, 1940.

SCHEFTELOWITZ, ISIDOR. *Die Zeit als Schicksalsgottheit in der indischen und iranischen Religion.* Stuttgart, 1929.

SCHWEITZER, BERNHARD. *Herakles.* Tübingen, 1922.

SÉBILLOT, PAUL. *Le Folk-lore de France.* Paris, 1904-1906. 4 vols.

SEDLMAYR, HANS. "Architektur als abbildende Kunst," *Österreichische Akademie der Wissenschaften* (Vienna), *Phil.-hist Klasse, Sitzungsberichte,* 225/3, (1948).

———. *Die Kathedrale.* Zurich, 1950.

SLAWIK, ALEXANDER. "Kultische Geheimbünde der Japaner und Germanen," *Wiener Beiträge zur Kulturgeschichte und Linguistik* (Salzburg and Leipzig), IV (1936), 675–764.

SOROKIN, PITIRIM A. *Contemporary Sociological Theories.* New York, 1928.

———. *Social and Cultural Dynamics.* New York, 1937–41, 4 vols.

STEVENS, E. S. *See* DROWER, E. S.

STEVENSON, (Margaret), MRS. SINCLAIR. *The Heart of Jainism.* London, 1915.

———. *The Rites of the Twice-Born.* London, 1920.

THOMPSON, CAMPBELL. *Assyrian Medical Texts.* London, 1923.

THORNDIKE, LYNN. *A History of Magic and Experimental Science.* New York, 1929–41. 6 vols.

TOYNBEE, ARNOLD J. *A Study of History.* London, 1934–39. 6 vols.

VALLÉE POUSSIN. *See* LA VALLÉE POUSSIN, LOUIS DE.

VANNICELLI, LUIGI. *La religione dei Lolo.* Milan, 1944.

VINCENT, ALBERT. *La Religion des Judéo-Araméens d'Éléphantine.* Paris, 1937.

WEILL, RAYMOND. *Le Champs des roseaux et le champs des offrandes dans la religion funéraire et la religion générale.* Paris, 1936.

WENSINCK, A. J. *The Ideas of the Western Semites Concerning the Navel of the Earth.* Amsterdam, 1916.

————. "The Semitic New Year and the Origin of Eschatology," *Acta Orientalia* (Lund), I (1923), 158–99.

WHEELWRIGHT, MARY C. See HASTEEN KLAH.

WHITNEY, W. D., and LANMAN, C. R. (trans.). *Atharva-Veda.* (Harvard Oriental Series, VII, VIII.) Cambridge, Mass., 1905.

WIDENGREN, GEO. *King and Saviour.* Uppsala, 1947. 2 vols.

WIEGER, LÉON. *Histoire des croyances religieuses et des opinions philosophiques en Chine.* Hsien-hsien, 1922.

ZAEHNER, R. C. "Zurvanica," *Bulletin of the School of Oriental and African Studies,* IX (1937–39), 303 ff., 573 ff., 871 ff.

ZIMMERN, HEINRICH. "Zum babylonischen Neujahrsfest," *Berichte über die Verhandlungen der Königlich Sächsischen Gesellschaft der Wissenschaften* (Leipzig), *Phil.-hist. Klasse,* LVIII (1906), pp. 126–156 and LXX (1918), pp. 1–52.

ADDENDA

The following translations, available since the first edition, are cited in the second printing.

CORBIN, HENRY. "Le Temps cyclique . . ." = "Cyclical Time in Mazdaism and Ismailism," trans. Ralph Manheim, in *Man and Time.* (Papers from the Eranos Yearbooks, 3.) New York and London, 1957. (pp. 115–72.)

ELIADE, MIRCEA. *Le Chamanisme . . .* = *Shamanism: Archaic Techniques of Ecstasy.* Trans. Willard R. Trask. New York and London, 1964.

————. *Images et symboles* = *Images and Symbols: Studies in Religious Symbolism.* Trans. Philip Mairet. New York and London, 1961.

————. "Le Temps et l'éternité . . ." = "Time and Eternity in Indian Thought," trans. Ralph Manheim, in *Man and Time.* (Papers from the Eranos Yearbooks, 3.) New York and London, 1957. (pp. 173–200.)

————. *Traité d'histoire . . .* = *Patterns in Comparative Religion.* Trans. Rosemary Sheed. London and New York, 1958.

————. *Yoga: Immortality and Freedom.* Trans. Willard R. Trask.

New York and London, 1958. (A trans. of *Le Yoga: Immortalité et Liberté*, Paris, 1954.)

LEEUW, GERARDUS VAN DER. "Urzeit und Endzeit" = "Primordial Time and Final Time," trans. Ralph Manheim, in *Man and Time.* (Papers from the Eranos Yearbooks, 3.) New York and London, 1957. (pp. 324–50.)

PUECH, HENRI-CHARLES. "La Gnose . . ." = "Gnosis and Time," trans. Ralph Manheim, in *Man and Time.* (Papers from the Eranos Yearbooks, 3.) New York and London, 1957. (pp. 38–84.)

INDEX

A

Abegg, Emil, 114 n
ablutions, 53
aborigines, Australian, 21
Abraham, 108–10, 160
abudhyam/abudhyamānam, 19
actors, ritual combats between, 53,
  56, 69
acts, human, value of, 4–5, 34
Adam, 8, 14, 59; creation of, 16–17
Aeneas, 24
Aesculapius, 31
aesthetics, 32
aeva, 89 n
Africa, 21, 26, 40 n, 52
ages, cosmic, 113–16, 117–18, 122,
  124–27, 132, 134–37
Agni, 10–11, 23, 79
agriculture, 28, 142, 156; rites of,
  25–27, 60–61, 63–64, 69 n, 152
Ahriman, 125
Ahuramazda, 64
aiones, 89 n
Aitareya Brāhmaṇa, 32, 79
Akiba, Rabbi, 59 n
akîtu ceremony, 55–58, 61
Akkad, 55, 70
Alakamanda, 9
Alaric, 137
Albertus Magnus, 144, 145
al-Bīrūnī, *see* Bīrūnī
Albright, W. F., 14 n
Alexander I, Czar, 42–43

Alexander the Great, 38, 119, 123
alimentation, 35, 51, 60–61
Allah, 62
allgemeine Lebenserfahrung, 150
altars, 8, 10–11, 77, 78–80
Amazulu tribe, 21
America, 3; Indian tribes, 14 n, 21,
  33–34, 40 n, 72–73, 83–84, 88
Ammon, 31
amor fati, 153
anachronisms, 40–41
anakuklosis, 89 n
Anath, 108 n
Anaximander, 120
ancestors, 4, 6, 46–47, 72 n, 161;
  and archetypes of profane activities, 28–34; and archetypes of
  rituals, 21–22
Andrija, 40
animals, 22; freedom of, 90–91,
  155; funerary, 67, 70; lunar, 87;
  totemic or emblematic, 28
anthropogony, 22
anthropology, 85
Antoine, Jean Claude, 146 n
Anu, 84
Anunit, star, 6
Aori, 33, 36
aparvan, 19
apeiron, 120
apocalypses, 60, 66, 116, 124, 126,
  128; Jewish, 17; St. John (Revelation), 8–9; Syriac, of Baruch, 8

mēnōk, 6–7, 7 *n*
menos, 29
mensis, 86 *n*
Mephistopheles, 20 *n*
Meru, Mount, 12
Mesopotamia, 3, 6, 13, 16, 100–102, 106
messenger, 101, 102, 152
Messiah, 38, 127
Messianism, 60, 105–12, 127, 132
metacosmesis, 123, 134
metallurgy, 156
metanoia, 129
metaphysical concepts, archaic world, 3
metior, 86 *n*
Mexico, 14 *n*, 88
Michael of Potuka, St., 42
Middle Ages, 17, 129, 142–45
midrash, 17
Mihragān, 66
Mikula, 41
Milica, 41
Minucius Felix, 144
miracles, 160 *n*
Mishnah, 15
Mithra, festival of, 66
modern man, and history, 78, 141, 154–62
Moldavia, 39
Moloch, 108
monotheism, 104–5
monsters, 9, 20; and New Year ritual, 55–58, 59–60; three-headed, 29, 37, 40
months, symbolism of, 51–52, 55, 56, 58, 59, 61, 65, 77
moon: lunar year, 51, 52; mysticism, 64; myths, 86–88, 101–2
Moret, Alexandre, 30 *n*
Moses, 7, 103, 105
Mount of the Lands, 13

mountains: celestial archetypes of, 6, 9; sacred, 12–17
mourning, 56
Mowinckel, Sigmund Otto Plytt, 60
mundus, 15–16
Mungan-ngaua, 32
Murko, Matthias, 43, 44
Murshilish, 128
Mus, Paul, 78, 80 *n*
mysteries, 58
mythical time, 20–21
mythicization, 39–46
myths: and archetypes, *see* archetypes; cosmic, *see* cosmic cycles; eternal return, *see* eternal return; and history, 34–48; lunar, 86–88; New Year, *see* New Year; of origin, 84–85; and rituals, 22, 23–27

N

Nāgārjuna, 116 *n*
Napoleonic wars, 42–43
Nativity, 130
nature, 55, 59, 90, 154, 155, 157–58
Navajo Indians, 83–84
navel of the earth, 13, 16–17
navigators, English, 11
Nawrôz, 63–65, 66
Nebuchadrezzar, 38, 128
neikos, 120
Neo-Pythagoreanism, 119, 123, 133, 134
Neo-Stoicism, 119, 133
new birth, 11, 54, 80
New Guinea, 32–33, 36
New Testament, 9, 23, 143, 160
New Year, 36; American Indian ceremonies, 72–73; Babylonian ceremony, 55–58, 61, 65; beginning of, 51–52; ceremonies,